The *New* Daily Study Bible

The Acts
of the Apostles

The *New* Daily Study Bible

The Acts
of the Apostles

William Barclay

Westminster John Knox Press
LOUISVILLE • LONDON

First edition published in 1953 as *The Daily Study Bible: The Acts of the Apostles*
Revised edition published in 1975
This third edition fully revised and updated by Saint Andrew Press and published as
The New Daily Study Bible: The Acts of the Apostles in 2003

Published in the United States by
Westminster John Knox Press
Louisville, Kentucky

The Scripture quotations contained herein are from the New Revised Standard
Version of the Bible, Anglicized Edition, copyright 1989, 1995 by the Division
of Christian Education of the National Council of the Churches of Christ in the
United States of America, and are used by permission. All rights reserved.

PRINTED IN THE UNITED STATES OF AMERICA

03 04 05 06 07 08 09 10 11 12 – 10 9 8 7 6 5 4 3 2 1

Library of Congress Cataloging-in-Publication Data is on file at the
Library of Congress, Washington, D.C.

ISBN 0–664–22675–2

In Grateful Memory of

W. D. B. and B. L. B.

from whose lips I first heard

the Name of Jesus

and in whose lives

I first saw Him

CONTENTS

ACTS

ACTS

ACTS

SERIES FOREWORD
(by Ronnie Barclay)

My father always had a great love for the English language
and its literature. As a student at the University of Glasgow,
he won a prize in the English class – and I have no doubt
that he could have become a Professor of English instead
of Divinity and Biblical Criticism. In a pre-computer age, he
had a mind like a computer that could store vast numbers of
quotations, illustrations, anecdotes and allusions; and, more
remarkably still, he could retrieve them at will. The editor of
this revision has, where necessary, corrected and attributed
the vast majority of these quotations with considerable skill
and has enhanced our pleasure as we read quotations from
Plato to T. S. Eliot.

There is another very welcome improvement in the new
text. My mother was one of five sisters, and my grandmother
was a commanding figure as the Presbyterian minister's
wife in a small village in Ayrshire in Scotland. She ran that
small community very efficiently, and I always felt that my
father, surrounded by so many women, was more than some-
what overawed by it all! I am sure that this is the reason why
his use of English tended to be dominated by the words 'man',
'men' and so on, with the result that it sounded very male-
orientated. Once again, the editor has very skilfully improved
my father's English and made the text much more readable
for all of us by amending the often one-sided language.

It is a well-known fact that William Barclay wrote at break-
neck speed and never corrected anything once it was on

paper – he took great pride in mentioning this at every possible opportunity! This revision, in removing repetition and correcting the inevitable errors that had slipped through, has produced a text free from all the tell-tale signs of very rapid writing. It is with great pleasure that I commend this revision to readers old and new in the certainty that William Barclay speaks even more clearly to us all with his wonderful appeal in this new version of his much-loved *Daily Study Bible*.

Ronnie Barclay
Bedfordshire
2001

GENERAL INTRODUCTION

(by William Barclay, from the 1975 edition)

The Daily Study Bible series has always had one aim – to convey the results of scholarship to the ordinary reader. A. S. Peake delighted in the saying that he was a 'theological middle-man', and I would be happy if the same could be said of me in regard to these volumes. And yet the primary aim of the series has never been academic. It could be summed up in the famous words of Richard of Chichester's prayer – to enable men and women 'to know Jesus Christ more clearly, to love him more dearly, and to follow him more nearly'.

It is all of twenty years since the first volume of *The Daily Study Bible* was published. The series was the brain-child of the late Rev. Andrew McCosh, MA, STM, the then Secretary and Manager of the Committee on Publications of the Church of Scotland, and of the late Rev. R. G. Macdonald, OBE, MA, DD, its Convener.

It is a great joy to me to know that all through the years *The Daily Study Bible* has been used at home and abroad, by minister, by missionary, by student and by layman, and that it has been translated into many different languages. Now, after so many printings, it has become necessary to renew the printer's type and the opportunity has been taken to restyle the books, to correct some errors in the text and to remove some references which have become outdated. At the same time, the Biblical quotations within the text have been changed to use the Revised Standard Version, but my own original translation of the New Testament passages has been retained at the beginning of each daily section.

There is one debt which I would be sadly lacking in courtesy if I did not acknowledge. The work of revision and correction has been done entirely by the Rev. James Martin, MA, BD, Minister of High Carntyne Church, Glasgow. Had it not been for him this task would never have been undertaken, and it is impossible for me to thank him enough for the selfless toil he has put into the revision of these books.

It is my prayer that God may continue to use *The Daily Study Bible* to enable men better to understand His word.

William Barclay
Glasgow
1975
(Published in the 1975 edition)

GENERAL FOREWORD

(by John Drane)

I only met William Barclay once, not long after his retirement from the chair of Biblical Criticism at the University of Glasgow. Of course I had known about him long before that, not least because his theological passion – the Bible – was also a significant formative influence in my own life and ministry. One of my most vivid memories of his influence goes back to when I was working on my own doctoral research in the New Testament. It was summer 1971, and I was a leader on a mission team working in the north-east of Scotland at the same time as Barclay's Baird Lectures were being broadcast on national television. One night, a young Ph.D. scientist who was interested in Christianity, but still unsure about some things, came to me and announced: 'I've just been watching William Barclay on TV. He's convinced me that I need to be a Christian; when can I be baptized?' That kind of thing did not happen every day. So how could it be that Barclay's message was so accessible to people with no previous knowledge or experience of the Christian faith?

I soon realised that there was no magic ingredient that enabled this apparently ordinary professor to be a brilliant communicator. His secret lay in who he was, his own sense of identity and purpose, and above all his integrity in being true to himself and his faith. Born in the far north of Scotland, he was brought up in Motherwell, a steel-producing town south of Glasgow where his family settled when he was only five, and this was the kind of place where he felt most at home. Though his association with the University of Glasgow provided a focus for his life over almost fifty years, from his first day as a student in 1925 to his retirement from the faculty in 1974, he never became an ivory-tower academic, divorced from the realities of life in the real world. On the contrary, it was his commitment to the working-class culture of industrial Clydeside that enabled him to make such a lasting contribution not only to the world of the university but also to the life of the Church.

He was ordained to the ministry of the Church of Scotland at the age of twenty-six, but was often misunderstood even by other Christians. I doubt that William Barclay would ever have chosen words such as 'missionary' or 'evangelist' to describe his own ministry, but he accomplished what few others have done, as he took the traditional Presbyterian emphasis on spirituality-through-learning and transformed it into a most effective vehicle for evangelism. His own primary interest was in the history and language of the New Testament, but William Barclay was never only a historian or literary critic. His constant concern was to explore how these ancient books, and the faith of which they spoke, could continue to be relevant to people of his own time. If the Scottish churches had known how to capitalize on his enormous popularity in the media during the 1960s and 1970s, they might easily have avoided much of the decline of subsequent years.

Connecting the Bible to life has never been the way to win friends in the world of academic theology, and Barclay could undoubtedly have made things easier for himself had he been prepared to be a more conventional academic. But he was too deeply rooted in his own culture – and too seriously committed to the gospel – for that. He could see little purpose in a belief system that was so wrapped up in arcane and complicated terminology that it was accessible only to experts. Not only did he demystify Christian theology, but he also did it for working people, addressing the kind of things that mattered to ordinary folks in their everyday lives. In doing so, he also challenged the elitism that has often been deeply ingrained in the twin worlds of academic theology and the Church, with their shared assumption that popular culture is an inappropriate vehicle for serious thinking. Professor Barclay can hardly have been surprised when his predilection for writing books for the masses – not to mention talking to them on television – was questioned by his peers and even occasionally dismissed as being 'unscholarly' or insufficiently 'academic'. That was all untrue, of course, for his work was soundly based in reliable scholarship and his own extensive knowledge of the original languages of the Bible. But like One many centuries before him (and unlike most of his peers, in both Church and academy), 'the common people heard him gladly' (Mark 12:37), which no doubt explains why his writings are still inspirational – and why it is a particular pleasure for me personally to commend them to a new readership in a new century.

John Drane
University of Aberdeen
2001

EDITOR'S PREFACE
(by Linda Foster)

When the first volume of the original *Daily Bible Readings*, which later became *The Daily Study Bible* (the commentary on Acts), was published in 1953, no one could have anticipated or envisaged the revolution in the use of language which was to take place in the last quarter of the twentieth century. Indeed, when the first revised edition, to which William Barclay refers in his General Introduction, was completed in 1975, such a revolution was still waiting in the wings. But at the beginning of the twenty-first century, inclusive language and the concept of political correctness are well-established facts of life. It has therefore been with some trepidation that the editing of this unique and much-loved text has been undertaken in producing *The New Daily Study Bible*. Inevitably, the demands of the new language have resulted in the loss of some of Barclay's most sonorous phrases, perhaps best remembered in the often-repeated words 'many a man'. Nonetheless, this revision is made in the conviction that William Barclay, the great communicator, would have welcomed it. In the discussion of Matthew 9:16–17 ('The Problem of the New Idea'), he affirmed the value of language that has stood the test of time and in which people have 'found comfort and put their trust', but he also spoke of 'living in a changing and expanding world' and questioned the wisdom of reading God's word to twentieth-century men and women in Elizabethan English. It is the intention of this new edition to heed that warning and to bring

William Barclay's message of God's word to readers of the twenty-first century in the language of their own time.

In the editorial process, certain decisions have been made in order to keep a balance between that new language and the familiar Barclay style. Quotations from the Bible are now taken from the New Revised Standard Version, but William Barclay's own translation of individual passages has been retained throughout. Where the new version differs from the text on which Barclay originally commented, because of the existence of an alternative reading, the variant text is indicated by square brackets. I have made no attempt to guess what Barclay would have said about the NRSV text; his commentary still refers to the Authorized (King James) and Revised Standard Versions of the Bible, but I believe that the inclusive language of the NRSV considerably assists the flow of the discussion.

For similar reasons, the dating conventions of BC and AD – rather than the more recent and increasingly used BCE (before the common era) and CE (common era) – have been retained. William Barclay took great care to explain the meanings of words and phrases and scholarly points, but it has not seemed appropriate to select new terms and make such explanations on his behalf.

One of the most difficult problems to solve has concerned monetary values. Barclay had his own system for translating the coinage of New Testament times into British currency. Over the years, these equivalent values have become increasingly out of date, and often the force of the point being made has been lost or diminished. There is no easy way to bring these equivalents up to date in a way that will continue to make sense, particularly when readers come from both sides of the Atlantic. I have therefore followed the only known yardstick that gives any feel for the values concerned, namely that a *denarius* was a day's wage for a working man, and I have made alterations to the text accordingly.

One of the striking features of *The Daily Study Bible* is the range of quotations from literature and hymnody that are used by way of illustration. Many of these passages appeared without identification or attribution, and for the new edition I have attempted wherever possible to provide sources and authors. In the same way, details have been included about scholars and other individuals cited, by way of context and explanation, and I am most grateful to Professor John Drane for his assistance in discovering information about some of the more obscure or unfamiliar characters. It is clear that readers use *The Daily Study Bible* in different ways. Some look up particular passages while others work through the daily readings in a more systematic way. The descriptions and explanations are therefore not offered every time an individual is mentioned (in order to avoid repetition that some may find tedious), but I trust that the information can be discovered without too much difficulty.

Finally, the 'Further Reading' lists at the end of each volume have been removed. Many new commentaries and individual studies have been added to those that were the basis of William Barclay's work, and making a selection from that ever-increasing catalogue is an impossible task. It is nonetheless my hope that the exploration that begins with these volumes of *The New Daily Study Bible* will go on in the discovery of new writers and new books.

Throughout the editorial process, many conversations have taken place – conversations with the British and American publishers, and with those who love the books and find in them both information and inspiration. Ronnie Barclay's contribution to this revision of his father's work has been invaluable. But one conversation has dominated the work, and that has been a conversation with William Barclay himself through the text. There has been a real sense of listening to his voice in all the questioning and in the searching for new words to convey the meaning of that text. The aim of *The New Daily Study Bible* is to make clear his message, so that the distinctive voice, which has spoken to so many in past years, may continue to be heard for generations to come.

Linda Foster
London
2001

INTRODUCTION TO THE
ACTS OF THE APOSTLES

A Precious Book

In one sense, Acts is the most important book in the New Testament. It is the simple truth that, if we did not possess Acts, we would have no information whatever about the early Church apart from what we could deduce from the letters of Paul.

There are two ways of writing history. There is the way which attempts to trace the course of events from week to week and from day to day; and there is the way which, as it were, opens a series of windows and gives us vivid glimpses of the great moments and personalities of any period. The second way is the way of Acts.

We usually speak of the Acts of the Apostles. But the book neither gives nor claims to give an exhaustive account of the acts of the apostles. Apart from Paul, only three apostles are mentioned in it. In Acts 12:2, we are told in one brief sentence that James, the brother of John, was executed by Herod. John appears in the narrative, but never speaks. It is only about Peter that the book gives any real information – and very soon, as a leading player, he passes from the scene. In the Greek, there is no 'The' before Acts; the correct title is Acts of Apostolic Men; and what Acts aims to do is to give us a series of typical exploits of the heroic figures of the early Church.

The Writer of the Book

Although the book never says so, from the earliest times Luke has been held to be its writer. About Luke, we really know very little; there are only three references to him in the New Testament – Colossians 4:14, Philemon 24 and 2 Timothy 4:11. From these, we can say two things with certainty. First, Luke was a doctor; second, he was one of Paul's most valued helpers and most loyal friends, for he was a companion of Paul in his last imprisonment. We can deduce the fact that he was a Gentile. Colossians 4:11 concludes a list of mentions and greetings from those who are 'of the circumcision', that is, from Jews; verse 12 begins a new list, and we naturally conclude that the new list is of Gentiles. So we have the very interesting fact that Luke is the only Gentile author in the New Testament.

We could have guessed that Luke was a doctor because of his instinctive use of medical words. In Luke 4:35, in telling of the man who had the spirit of an unclean devil, he says: 'When the demon had thrown him down' and uses the correct medical word for convulsions. In Luke 9:38, when he draws the picture of the man who asked Jesus: 'I beg you to look at my son', he employs the conventional word for a doctor paying a visit to a patient. The most interesting example is in the saying about the camel and the needle's eye. All three of the writers of what have come to be known as the synoptic gospels give us that saying (Matthew 19:24; Mark 10:25; Luke 18:25). For *needle*, both Mark and Matthew use the Greek *raphis*, the ordinary word for a tailor's or a household needle. Luke alone uses *belonē*, the technical word for a surgeon's needle. Luke was a doctor, and a doctor's words came most naturally to his pen.

ACTS

The Recipient of the Book

Luke wrote both his gospel and Acts to a man called Theophilus (Luke 1:3; Acts 1:1). We can only guess who Theophilus was. Luke 1:3 calls him 'most excellent Theophilus'. The phrase really means 'Your Excellency' and indicates a man high up in the service of the Roman government. There are three possibilities.

(1) Just possibly, Theophilus is not a real name at all. In those days, it might well have been dangerous to be a Christian. *Theophilus* comes from two Greek words – *theos*, which means *God*, and *philein*, which means *to love*. It may be that Luke wrote to someone who loved God, whose real name he did not mention for safety's sake.

(2) If Theophilus was a real person, he must have been a high government official. Perhaps Luke wrote to show him that Christianity was a lovely thing and that Christians were good people. Maybe his writing was an attempt to persuade a government official not to persecute Christians.

(3) There is a more romantic theory than either of these, based on the facts that Luke was a doctor and that doctors in the ancient days were often slaves. It has been suggested that Luke was the doctor of Theophilus, that Theophilus had been gravely ill, that by Luke's skill and devotion he was brought back to health, and that in gratitude he gave Luke his freedom. Then, it may be, Luke wanted to show how grateful he was for this gift; and, since the most precious thing he had was the story of Jesus, he wrote it down and sent it to his benefactor.

Luke's Aim in Writing Acts

Anyone who writes a book does so for a reason, and maybe for more than one reason. Let us now consider why Luke wrote Acts.

(1) One of his reasons was to commend Christianity to the Roman government. Again and again, he goes out of his way to show how courteous Roman magistrates were to Paul. In Acts 13:12, Sergius Paulus, the governor of Cyprus, becomes a Christian. In 18:12ff., Gallio is absolutely fair-minded in Corinth. In 16:35ff., the magistrates at Philippi discover their mistake and apologize publicly to Paul. In 19:31, the Asiarchs in Ephesus are shown to be concerned that no harm should come to Paul. Luke was pointing out that, in the years before he wrote, Roman officials had often been well-disposed and always just and fair to Christianity.

Further, Luke takes pains to show that Christians were good and loyal citizens and had always been regarded as such. In Acts 18:14, Gallio declares that there is no question of crime or villainy. In 19:37, the secretary of Ephesus gives the Christians a good report. In 23:29, Claudius Lysias is careful to say that he has nothing against Paul. In 25:25, Festus declares that Paul has done nothing worthy of death, and in the same chapter Festus and Agrippa agree that Paul might well have been released had he not appealed to Caesar.

Luke was writing in the days when Christians were disliked and persecuted; and he told his story in such a way as to show that the Roman magistrates had always been perfectly fair to Christianity and that they had never regarded the Christians as evil. In fact, the very interesting suggestion has been made that Acts is nothing other than the brief prepared for Paul's defence when he stood trial before the Roman emperor.

(2) One of Luke's aims was to show that Christianity was for all people of every country. This was one of the things the Jews found it hard to grasp. They had the idea that they were God's chosen people and that God had no use for any other nation. Luke sets out to prove otherwise. He shows

Philip preaching to the Samaritans; he shows Stephen making Christianity universal and being killed for it; he shows Peter accepting Cornelius into the Church; he shows the Christians preaching to the Gentiles at Antioch; he shows Paul travelling far and wide winning men and women of every kind for Christ; and in Acts 15 he shows the Church making the great decision to accept the Gentiles on equal terms with the Jews.

(3) But these were merely secondary aims. Luke's chief purpose is set out in the words of the risen Christ in 1:8: 'You will be my witnesses in Jerusalem, in all Judaea and Samaria, and to the ends of the earth.' It was to show the expansion of Christianity – to show how that religion which began in a little corner of Palestine had in not much more than thirty years reached Rome.

The Church historian C. H. Turner has pointed out that Acts falls into six panels, each ending with what might be called a progress report. The six panels are:

(a) 1:1–6:7; this tells of the church at Jerusalem and the preaching of Peter; and it finishes with the summary: 'The word of God continued to spread; the number of the disciples increased greatly in Jerusalem, and a great many of the priests became obedient to the faith.'

(b) 6:8–9:31; this describes the spread of Christianity through Palestine and the martyrdom of Stephen, followed by the preaching in Samaria. It ends with the summary: 'Meanwhile the church throughout Judaea, Galilee and Samaria had peace and was built up. Living in the fear of the Lord and in the comfort of the Holy Spirit, it increased in numbers.'

(c) 9:32–12:24; this includes the conversion of Paul, the extension of the Church to Antioch, and the reception of Cornelius, the Gentile, into the Church by Peter. Its summary is: 'The word of God continued to advance.'

(d) 12:25–16:5; this tells of the extension of the Church through Asia Minor and the preaching tour of Galatia. It ends: 'So the churches were strengthened in the faith and increased in numbers daily.'

(e) 16:6–19:20; this describes the extension of the Church to Europe and the work of Paul in great Gentile cities like Corinth and Ephesus. Its summary runs: 'So the word of the Lord grew mightily and prevailed.'

(f) 19:21–28:31; this tells of the arrival of Paul in Rome and his imprisonment there. It ends with the picture of Paul 'proclaiming the kingdom of God and teaching about the Lord Jesus Christ with all boldness and without hindrance'.

This plan of Acts answers its most puzzling question – why does it finish where it does? It finishes with Paul in prison awaiting judgment. We would so much have liked to know what happened to him; and the end remains a mystery. But Luke stopped there because he had achieved his purpose; he had shown how Christianity began in Jerusalem and swept across the world until it reached Rome. One New Testament scholar has said that the title of Acts might be: 'How they brought the Good News from Jerusalem to Rome.'

Luke's Sources

Luke was a historian, and the sources from which a historian draws information are all important. Where then did Luke get his facts? In this connection, Acts falls into two parts.

(1) There are the first fifteen chapters, describing events of which Luke had no personal knowledge. He most probably had access to two sources.

(a) There were the records of the local churches. They may never have been set down in writing, but the churches had their stories. In this section, we can distinguish three records. There is the record of the *Jerusalem church*, which we find in chapters 1–5 and in chapters 15–16. There is the record of the *church at Caesarea*, which covers 8:26–40 and 9:31–10:48. There is the record of the *church at Antioch*, which includes 11:19–30 and 12:25–14:28.

(b) It is very likely that there were cycles of stories which were the Acts of Peter, the Acts of John, the Acts of Philip and the Acts of Stephen. Beyond a doubt, Luke's friendship with Paul would bring him into touch with all the great figures of all the churches, and all their stories would be at his disposal.

(2) There are chapters 16–28. Luke had personal knowledge of much that is included in this section. When we read Acts carefully, we notice a strange thing. Most of the time, Luke's narrative is in the third-person plural; but in certain passages it changes over to the first-person plural, and 'they' becomes 'we'. The 'we' passages are as follows: Acts 16:10–17, 20:5–16, 21:1–18 and 27:1–28:16. On all these occasions, Luke must have been present. He must have kept a travel diary, and in these passages we have eyewitness accounts. As for the times when he was not present, many were the hours he must have spent in prison with Paul, and many were the stories Paul must have told him, There can have been no great figure Luke did not know, and in every case he must have got his story from someone who was there.

When we read Acts, we may be quite sure that no historian ever had better sources or used those sources more accurately.

THE ACTS OF THE APOSTLES

POWER TO GO ON

Acts 1:1–5

> My Dear Theophilus, I have already given you an
> account of all the things that Jesus began to do and to
> teach, right up to the day when he was taken up to
> heaven, after he had, through the Holy Spirit, given his
> instructions to the apostles whom he had chosen. In the
> days that followed his sufferings, he also showed himself
> living to them by many proofs, for he was seen by them
> on various occasions throughout a period of forty days;
> and he spoke to them about the kingdom of God. While
> he was staying with them, he told them not to go away
> from Jerusalem but to wait for the Father's promise,
> 'which', he said, 'I told you about; for I told you that
> John baptized with water but you will be baptized with
> the Holy Spirit before many days have passed'.

In two senses, Acts is the second chapter of a continued
story. First, it is the second volume which Luke had sent to
Theophilus. In the first volume, his gospel, Luke had told the
story of the earthly life of Jesus. Now he goes on to tell the
story of the Christian Church. Second, Acts is the second
volume of a story which has no end. The gospel was only the
story of what Jesus *began* to do and to teach.

There are different kinds of immortality. There is an *immortality of fame*. In *Henry V*, Shakespeare puts into the king's mouth a speech which promises an immortal memory if the Battle of Agincourt is won:

> This story shall the good man tell his son;
> And Crispin Crispian shall ne'er go by,
> From this day to the ending of the world,
> But we in it shall be remembered.

Beyond a doubt, Jesus did win such an immortality, for his name will never be forgotten.

There is an *immortality of influence*. Some people leave an effect in the world which cannot die. Sir Francis Drake was the greatest of English sailors, and to this day the Royal Naval Barracks at Plymouth are called *HMS Drake* so that there may always be sailors armed with 'that crested and prevailing name'. Without a doubt, Jesus won an immortality of influence, for his effect upon the world and lives of men and women cannot die.

Above all, there is an *immortality of presence and of power*. Jesus not only left an immortal name and influence; he is still alive and still active. He is not the one who *was*; he is the one who *is*.

In one sense, it is the whole lesson of Acts that the life of Jesus goes on *in his Church*. Professor John Foster of Glasgow University told how an inquirer from Hinduism came to an Indian bishop. Without any help, he had read the New Testament. The story had fascinated him, and Christ had laid his spell upon him. 'Then he read on . . . and felt he had entered into a new world. In the gospels it was Jesus, his works and his suffering. In the Acts . . . what the disciples did and thought and taught had taken the place that Christ had occupied. The Church continued where Jesus had left off at his death.

"Therefore," said this man to me, "I must belong to *the Church that carries on the life of Christ.*"' The book of Acts tells of the Church that carries on the life of Christ.

This passage tells us how the Church was empowered to do that by the work of the Holy Spirit. We often call the Holy Spirit the Comforter. That word goes back to the translation by John Wyclif, made in the fourteenth century; but in Wyclif's day it had a different meaning. It comes from the Latin *fortis*, which means *brave*; the Comforter is the one who fills people with courage and with strength. In the book of Acts, indeed all through the New Testament, it is very difficult to draw a line between the work of the Spirit and the work of the risen Christ; and we do not need to do so, for the coming of the Spirit is the fulfilment of the promise of Jesus: 'And remember, I am with you always, to the end of the age' (Matthew 28:20).

Let us note one other thing. The apostles were told to *wait* for the coming of the Spirit. We would gain more power and courage and peace if we learned to wait. In the business of life, we need to learn to be still. 'Those who wait for the Lord shall renew their strength' (Isaiah 40:31). Amid life's surging activity, there must be time to receive.

THE KINGDOM AND ITS WITNESSES

Acts 1:6–8

> So when they had met together, they asked him: 'Lord, are you going to restore the kingdom of Israel at this time?' But he said to them: 'It is not yours to know the times and the seasons which the Father has appointed by his own authority. But when the Holy Spirit has come upon you, you will receive power; and you will be my witnesses both in Jerusalem and in all Judaea and in Samaria and to the furthest bounds of the earth.'

THROUGHOUT his ministry, Jesus laboured under one great disadvantage. The centre of his message was *the kingdom* of God (Mark 1:14); but he meant one thing by the kingdom, and those who listened to him meant another.

The Jews were always vividly conscious of being God's chosen people. They took that to mean that they were destined for special privilege and for worldwide power. The whole course of their history proved that, humanly speaking, that could never be. Palestine was a little country not more than 120 miles long by 40 miles wide. It had its days of independence, but it had become subject in turn to the Babylonians, the Persians, the Greeks and the Romans. So the Jews began to look forward to a day when God would break directly into human history and establish that world sovereignty of which they dreamed. They thought of the kingdom in political terms.

How did Jesus see it? Let us look at the Lord's Prayer. In it, there are two petitions side by side. 'Your kingdom come; your will be done on earth as it is in heaven.' It is characteristic of Hebrew style, as any verse of the Psalms will show, to say things in two parallel forms, the second of which repeats or amplifies the first. That is what these two petitions do. The second is a definition of the first. Therefore, we see that, by *the kingdom*, Jesus meant a society upon earth where God's will would be as perfectly done as it is in heaven. Because of that, it would be a kingdom founded on love and not on power.

To achieve that, men and women needed the Holy Spirit. Twice already, Luke has talked about waiting for the coming of the Spirit. We are not to think that the Spirit came into existence at this point for the first time. It is quite possible for a power always to exist but for people to experience or take it at some given moment. For instance, no one invented atomic power. It always existed; but it was not until the middle of the twentieth century that anyone was able to access that power. So God is eternally Father, Son and Holy Spirit; but there came a special time when people experienced to the full that power which had always been present.

The power of the Spirit was going to make them Christ's witnesses. That witness was to operate in an ever-extending series of concentric circles – first in Jerusalem, then throughout Judaea; then Samaria, the semi-Jewish state, would be a kind of bridge leading out into the world beyond Israel; and finally this witness was to go out to the ends of the earth.

Let us note certain things about this Christian witness. First, a witness is someone who says: 'I know this is true.' In a court of law, hearsay is not accepted as evidence; witnesses must give an account of their own personal experiences. A witness does not say 'I think so', but 'I know.'

Second, the real witness is not of words but of deeds. When the journalist Sir Henry Morton Stanley had discovered David Livingstone in central Africa and had spent some time with him, he said: 'If I had been with him any longer, I would have been compelled to be a Christian – and he never spoke to me about it at all.' The witness of Livingstone's life was irresistible.

Third, in Greek, the word for *witness* and the word for *martyr* is the same (*martus*). A witness had to be ready to become a martyr. To be a witness means to be loyal whatever the cost.

THE GLORY OF DEPARTURE
AND THE GLORY OF RETURN

Acts 1:9–11

> When he had said these things, while they were watching, he was taken up and a cloud received him

13

> and he passed from their sight. While they were gazing into heaven, as he went upon his way, behold, two men in white garments stood beside them; and they said to them: 'Men of Galilee, why are you standing looking up into heaven? This Jesus who has been taken up into heaven from you will come again in the same way as you have seen him go to heaven.'

THIS short passage leaves us face to face with two of the most difficult ideas in the New Testament.

First, it tells of the ascension. Only Luke tells this story; and he has already given an account of it in his gospel (Luke 24:50–3). For two reasons, the ascension was an absolute necessity. One was that there had to be a final moment when Jesus went back to the glory which was his. The forty days of the resurrection appearances had passed. Clearly, that was a time which was unique and could not go on forever. Equally clearly, the end to that period had to be definite. There would have been something quite wrong if the resurrection appearances had just simply petered out.

For the second reason, we must transport ourselves in imagination back to the time when this happened. Nowadays, we do not regard heaven as some place located beyond the sky; we regard it as a state of blessedness when we will be with God for all time. But in those days everyone, even the wisest, thought of the earth as flat and of heaven as a place above the sky. Therefore, if Jesus was to give his followers undeniable proof that he had returned to his glory, the ascension was absolutely necessary. But we must note this. When Luke tells of this in his gospel, he says: 'they . . . returned to Jerusalem with great joy' (Luke 24:52). In spite of the ascension, or maybe because of it, the disciples were quite sure that Jesus had not gone from them but that he was with them forever.

Second, this passage brings us face to face with the second coming. We must remember two things about the second coming. First, to speculate when and how it will happen is both foolish and useless, as Jesus said that not even he knew the day and the hour when the Son of Man would come (Mark 13:32). There is something almost blasphemous in speculating about something which was hidden from even Christ himself. Second, the essential teaching of Christianity is that God has a plan for us and the world. We are bound to believe that history is not a haphazard conglomeration of chance events which are going nowhere. We are bound to believe that there is some divine far-off event to which the whole creation moves and that, when that final fulfilment comes, Jesus Christ will be Judge and Lord of all. The second coming is not a matter for speculation and for a curiosity that is quite out of place; it is a summons to make ourselves ready for that day when it comes.

THE FATE OF THE TRAITOR

Acts 1:12–20

Then they made their way back to Jerusalem from the hill which is called the Mount of Olives, which is near Jerusalem, about half a mile away. When they came in, they went up to the upper room where they were staying; Peter and John and James and Andrew, Philip and Thomas, Bartholomew and Matthew, James the son of Alphaeus and Simon the Zealot and Judas the son of James were there. All of them with one united heart persevered in prayer, together with certain women and with Mary, Jesus' mother and with his brothers.

And in these days Peter stood up among the brethren and said – the number of people who were together was about 120 – 'Brethren, the Scripture had to be fulfilled, which the Holy Spirit foretold through the mouth of David about Judas who was guide to those who arrested Jesus, because he was one of our number and had received his allotted part in our service. (This man bought a piece of ground with the proceeds of his wicked deed; and he fell headlong and burst asunder and his bowels gushed out. This became a well-known fact to all those who lived in Jerusalem so that the piece of ground was called in their language Akeldama, which means the place of blood.) For it stands written in the book of Psalms: "Let the place where he lodged be desolate and let no one stay in it." And: "Let another receive his office." '

BEFORE we come to the fate of the traitor Judas, there are certain things we may notice in this passage. For the Jews, the Sabbath was entirely a day of rest when all work was forbidden. A journey was limited to 2,000 cubits, and that distance was called a Sabbath day's journey. A cubit was eighteen inches; so a Sabbath day's journey was rather more than half a mile.

It is interesting to note that Jesus' brothers are here with the company of the disciples. During Jesus' lifetime, they had been among his opponents (Mark 3:21). It may well be that for them, as for so many others, the death of Jesus opened their eyes and penetrated their hearts in a way that even his life could not do.

We are told that the number of the disciples was about 120. That is one of the most uplifting things in the New Testament. There were only 120 pledged to Christ, and it is very unlikely that any of them had ever been outside the narrow confines of Palestine – but these 120 ordinary men and women were told to go out and evangelize the whole world. If ever anything began from small beginnings, the Christian Church did. We may well be the only Christians in our shop, our factory, our office, in our circle of family and friends. These disciples gallantly faced their task, and so must we; and it may be that we too will be the small beginning from which the kingdom in our area of life will spread.

The great interest of this passage is the fate of Judas. What exactly the Greek means here is uncertain; but in Matthew's account (Matthew 27:3–5) we are left in no doubt that Judas committed suicide. It must always be a matter of speculation why Judas betrayed Jesus. Various suggestions have been put forward.

(1) It has been suggested that *Iscariot* means *man of Kerioth*. If it does, Judas was the only non-Galilaean among the apostles. It may be that he felt himself the odd one out and grew so embittered that he did this terrible thing.

(2) It may be that Judas became an informer to save his own skin and then saw the enormity of what he had done.

(3) It may be that he did it simply out of greed for money. If he did, it was the most dreadful bargain in history – for he sold his Lord for thirty pieces of silver, which was the equivalent of a little under six months' pay for the average worker.

(4) It may be that Judas came to hate Jesus. From others he could disguise the evil intentions of his heart; but the eyes of Jesus could penetrate to the inmost corners of his being. It may be that in the end he was driven to destroy the one who knew him for what he was.

(5) It may be that *Iscariot* is a form of a Greek word which means a dagger-bearer. The 'dagger-bearers' were a band of violent nationalists who were prepared to undertake assassination and murder in a campaign to set Palestine free. Perhaps Judas saw in Jesus the very person who could lead the

nationalists to triumph; and, when he saw that Jesus refused that way, he turned against him and in his bitter disappointment betrayed him.

(6) It is likeliest of all that Judas never meant Jesus to die, but betrayed him with the intention of forcing his hand. If that is so, Judas had the tragic experience of seeing his plan go desperately wrong, and in his bitter remorse he committed suicide.

Whatever the reason for his actions, Judas goes down in history as the most wicked name of all. There can never be any peace for anyone who betrays Christ.

THE QUALIFICATIONS OF AN APOSTLE

Acts 1:21–6

> 'So then, of the men who were with us during all the time our Lord went in and out among us, beginning from the baptism of John until the day on which he was taken up from us – of these we must choose one to be a witness of the resurrection along with us.' So they selected two, Joseph, who was called Barsabbas, whose surname was Justus, and Matthias. Then they prayed and said: 'O Lord, who knowest the hearts of all, do thou show us which of these two thou hast chosen to take his place in this service and in the apostleship, from which Judas fell away and went to his own place.' So they made them draw lots and the lot fell on Matthias, and he was elected to be along with the eleven apostles.

WE look briefly at the method of choosing someone to take Judas' place among the apostles. It may seem strange to us that the method was that of casting lots. But among the Jews it was the natural thing to do, because all the offices and duties in the Temple were settled that way. The names of the candidates were written on stones; the stones were put into a jar, and the jar was shaken until one stone fell out; and the one whose name was on that stone was elected to office.

The great fact about this passage is that it gives us two supremely important truths.

First, it tells us that the *function of an apostle* was to be a witness to the resurrection. The real mark of Christians is not that they know about Jesus but that they know Jesus. The basic mistake in Christianity is to regard Jesus as someone who lived and died and whose life we study and whose story we read. Jesus is not a figure in a book, he is a living presence; and Christians are men and women whose lives are a witness to the fact that they know and have met the risen Lord.

Second, it tells us that the *qualification of an apostle* was that the person must have been with Jesus. The real Christian is the one who lives day by day with Jesus. It was said of the great preacher John Brown, the eighteenth-century minister of the Scottish town of Haddington, that often when he preached he paused as if listening for a voice. The writer Jerome K. Jerome tells of an old cobbler who, on the coldest day, left the door of his shop open. On being asked why, he replied: 'So that Jesus can come in if he is passing by.' We often speak about what would happen if Jesus were here and how differently we would live if he were in our homes and at our work. The daughter of the British politician W. H. Smith, Lady Emily Acland, tells how once her little daughter had a spasm of temper. Afterwards, she and the daughter were sitting on the stairs making up again, and the little girl said: 'I wish Jesus would come and stay in our house all the time.' But the fact is that Jesus *is* here; and real Christians are those who live all their lives with Christ.

THE DAY OF PENTECOST

WE may never know precisely what happened on the Day of Pentecost, but we do know that it was one of the supremely great days of the Christian Church – for, on that day, the Holy Spirit came to the Christian Church in a very special way.

Acts has been called the Gospel of the Holy Spirit; so, before we turn to detailed consideration of its second chapter, let us take a general view of what Acts has to say about the Holy Spirit.

The Coming of the Spirit

It is perhaps unfortunate that we so often speak of the events at Pentecost as the coming of the Holy Spirit. The danger is that we may think that the Holy Spirit came into existence at that time. That is not so; God is eternally Father, Son and Holy Spirit. In fact, Acts makes that quite clear. The Holy Spirit was speaking in David (Acts 1:16); the Spirit spoke through Isaiah (Acts 28:25); Stephen accuses the Jews of having opposed the Spirit all through their history (Acts 7:51). In that sense, the Spirit is God in every age revealing his truth. At the same time, something special happened at Pentecost.

The Work of the Spirit in Acts

From that moment, the Holy Spirit became the dominant reality in the life of the early Church.

For one thing, *the Holy Spirit was the source of all guidance*. The Spirit moves Philip to make contact with the Ethiopian eunuch (Acts 8:29), prepares Peter for the coming of the messengers from Cornelius (Acts 10:19), orders Peter to go without hesitation with these messengers (Acts 11:12), enables Agabus to foretell the coming famine (Acts 11:28), orders the setting apart of Paul and Barnabas for the momentous step of taking the gospel to the Gentiles (Acts 13:2, 13:4), guides the decisions of the Council of Jerusalem (Acts 15:28), guides Paul past Asia, Mysia and Bithynia, down into Troas and from there to Europe (Acts 16:6), and tells Paul what awaits him in Jerusalem (Acts 20:23). The early Church was a Spirit-guided community.

For another thing, *all the leaders of the Church were men of the Spirit*. The Seven are men of the Spirit (Acts 6:3); Stephen and Barnabas are full of the Spirit (Acts 7:55, 11:24). Paul tells the elders at Ephesus that it was the Spirit who made them overseers over the Church of God (Acts 20:28).

And further, *the Spirit was the source of day-to-day courage and power*. The disciples are to receive power when the Spirit comes (Acts 1:8); Peter's courage and eloquence before the Sanhedrin are the result of the activity of the Spirit (Acts 4:31); Paul's conquest of Elymas is the work of the Spirit (Acts 13:9). The Christian courage to meet the dangerous situation, the Christian power to cope with life more than adequately, the Christian eloquence when eloquence is needed, and the Christian joy which is independent of circumstances are all attributed to the work of the Spirit.

Finally, Acts 5:32 speaks of the Spirit 'whom God has given to those who obey him'. This has in it the great truth that *the degree to which we can possess the Spirit is conditioned by the kind of people we are*. It means that anyone who is honestly trying to do the will of God will experience more and more of the wonder of the Spirit.

In the first thirteen chapters of Acts, there are more than forty references to the Holy Spirit; the early Church was a Spirit-filled Church, and that was the source of its power.

THE BREATH OF GOD

Acts 2:1–13

> So when the day of Pentecost came round, they were all
> together in one place; and all of a sudden there came
> from heaven a sound like that of a violent, rushing wind,
> and it filled the whole house where they were sitting.
> And tongues, like tongues of fire, appeared to them,
> which distributed themselves among them and settled
> on each one of them. And they were all filled with the
> Holy Spirit, and they began to speak in other tongues as
> the Spirit gave them the power of utterance.
>
> There were, staying in Jerusalem, Jews, devout men
> from all the races under heaven. When the news of this
> got abroad, the crowd assembled and came pouring
> together; for each one of them heard them speaking in
> his own language. They were all astonished and kept
> saying in amazement: 'Look now! Are all these men
> who are speaking not Galilaeans? And how is it that
> each one of us hears them speaking in our own language
> in which we were born? Parthians and Medes, Elamites,
> those who live in Mesopotamia, in Judaea and Cappa-
> docia, in Pontus, in Asia, in Phrygia and Pamphylia, in
> Egypt and the parts of Libya round about Cyrene,
> Romans, who are staying here, Jews and proselytes,
> people from Crete and Arabia – we hear these men telling
> the wonders of God in our own tongues.' They were all
> astonished and did not know what to make of it, and
> they kept on saying to each other: 'What can this mean?'
> But others kept on saying in mockery: 'They are filled
> with new wine.'

THERE were three great Jewish festivals to which every male
Jew living within twenty miles of Jerusalem was legally
bound to come – the Passover, Pentecost and the Feast of

Tabernacles. Pentecost means 'the Fiftieth', and another name for Pentecost was 'the Feast of Weeks'. It was so called because it fell on the fiftieth day, a week of weeks, after the Passover. The Passover was celebrated in the middle of April; therefore Pentecost fell at the beginning of June. By that time, travelling conditions were at their best. At least as many came to the Feast of Pentecost as came to the Passover. That explains the list of countries mentioned in this chapter; never was there a more international crowd in Jerusalem than at the time of Pentecost.

The feast itself was significant in two ways. (1) It had a *historical* significance. It commemorated the giving of the law to Moses on Mount Sinai. (2) It had an *agricultural* significance. At the Passover, part of the first crop of barley was offered to God; and at Pentecost two loaves were offered in gratitude for the safe gathering in of the harvest. It had one other unique characteristic. The law laid it down that on that day people should not do their everyday work (Leviticus 23:21; Numbers 28:26). So it was a holiday for everyone, and the crowds on the streets would be greater than ever.

What happened at Pentecost we really do not know, except that the disciples had an experience of the power of the Spirit flooding their beings such as they had never had before. We must remember that, for this part of Acts, Luke was not an eyewitness. He tells the story as if the disciples had suddenly acquired the gift of speaking in *foreign* languages. For two reasons, that is not likely.

(1) There was in the early Church a phenomenon which has never completely disappeared. It was called *speaking with tongues* (cf. Acts 10:46, 19:6). The main passage which describes it is 1 Corinthians 14. What happened was that someone, in an ecstasy, began to pour out a flood of unintelligible

sounds in no known language. That was supposed to be directly inspired by the Spirit of God and was a gift greatly coveted. Paul did not approve of it, because he preferred that a message should be given in a language that could be understood. In fact, he said that a stranger coming in might well think that the members of the congregation were mad (1 Corinthians 14:23). That precisely fits Acts 2:13. People speaking in tongues might well appear to be drunk to someone who had never witnessed the phenomenon.

(2) To speak in foreign languages was unnecessary. The crowd was made up of Jews (verse 5) and converts (verse 10) – Gentiles who had accepted the Jewish religion and the Jewish way of life. For a crowd like that, at most two languages were necessary. Almost all Jews spoke Aramaic; and, even if they were Jews of the dispersion from a foreign land, they would speak the language which almost everyone in the world spoke at that time – Greek.

It seems most likely that Luke, a Gentile, had confused speaking with tongues with speaking in *foreign* languages. What happened was that, for the first time in their lives, this mixed crowd was hearing the word of God in a way that struck straight home to their hearts and that they could understand. The power of the Spirit was such that it had given the disciples a message that could reach every heart.

THE FIRST CHRISTIAN PREACHING

ACTS 2:14–42 is one of the most interesting passages in the New Testament, because it is an account of the first Christian sermon ever preached. In the early Church, there were four different kinds of preaching.

(1) There was *kerugma*. *Kerugma* literally means *a herald's announcement* and is the plain statement of the facts

24

of the Christian message, about which, as the early preachers saw it, there can be no argument or doubt.

(2) There was *didache*. *Didache* literally means *teaching*, and explained the meaning of the facts which had been proclaimed.

(3) There was *paraklēsis*, which literally means *exhortation*. This kind of preaching urged upon people the duty of fitting their lives to match the *kerugma* and the *didache* which had been given.

(4) There was *homilia*, which means the treatment of any subject or sphere of life in light of the Christian message.

Fully rounded preaching has something of all four elements. There is the plain proclamation of the facts of the Christian gospel; the explanation of the meaning and the relevance of these facts; the exhortation to fit life to them; and the treatment of all the activities of life in the light of the Christian message.

In Acts, we shall meet mainly with *kerugma*, because Acts tells of the proclamation of the facts of the gospel to those who had never heard them before. This *kerugma* follows a pattern which repeats itself over and over again all through the New Testament.

(1) There is the proof that Jesus and all that happened to him is the fulfilment of Old Testament prophecy. In recent years, less and less stress has been laid on the fulfilment of prophecy. We have come to see that the prophets were not nearly so much *foretellers* of events to come as *forthtellers* of God's truth. But this stress of early preaching on prophecy conserved the great truth that history is not haphazard and that there is meaning to it. To believe in the possibility of prophecy is to believe that God is in control and that he is working out his purposes.

(2) In Jesus the Messiah has come, the messianic prophecies are fulfilled and the new age has dawned. The early

25

Church had a tremendous sense that Jesus was the hinge of all history; that, with his coming, eternity had invaded time; and that, therefore, life and the world could never be the same again.

(3) The *kerugma* went on to state that Jesus had been born of the line of David, that he had taught, that he had worked miracles, that he had been crucified, that he had been raised from the dead and that he was now at the right hand of God. The early Church was sure that the Christian religion was based on the earthly life of Christ. But it was also certain that that earthly life and death were not the end and that after them came the resurrection. Jesus was not merely someone about whom they read or heard; he was someone whom they met and knew, a living presence.

(4) The early preachers went on to insist that Jesus would return in glory to establish his kingdom upon earth. In other words, the early Church believed intensely in the second coming. This doctrine has to some extent passed out of modern preaching; but it does conserve the truth that history is going somewhere and that some day there will be a completion and fulfilment and that people are therefore in the way or on the way.

(5) The preaching finished with the statement that only in Jesus was salvation possible, that those who believed on him would receive the Holy Spirit and that those who would not believe were destined for terrible things. That is to say, it finished with both a *promise* and a *threat*. It is exactly like that voice which John Bunyan heard, as if coming from right behind him, demanding: 'Wilt thou leave thy sins and go to heaven, or wilt thou have thy sins and go to hell?'

If we read through Peter's sermon as a whole, we will see how these five strands are woven into it.

GOD'S DAY HAS COME

Acts 2:14–21

> But Peter stood up with the eleven and raised his voice
> and said to them: 'You who are Jews and you who are
> staying in Jerusalem, let this be known to you and listen
> to my words. These men are not, as you suppose, drunk;
> for it is only 9 am. But this is what was spoken by our
> prophet Joel: "It will be in the last days, says God, that
> I will pour out from my Spirit upon all men, and your
> sons and your daughters will prophesy and your young
> men will see visions and your old men will dream
> dreams. And I will pour out from my Spirit upon my
> men servants and my maid servants in these days and
> they will prophesy. I will send wonders in the heaven
> above and signs upon the earth below, blood and fire
> and vapour of smoke. The sun will be changed into
> darkness and the moon into blood before there comes
> the great and famous day of the Lord. And it shall be
> that all whosoever shall call upon the name of the Lord
> shall be saved." '

THIS passage brings us face to face with one of the basic ideas
of both the Old and the New Testaments – that of *the day of
the Lord*. Much in both the Old and the New Testaments is
not fully intelligible unless we know the basic principles
underlying that belief.

The Jews never lost the conviction that they were God's
chosen people. They interpreted that status to mean that they
were chosen for special privilege among the nations. They
were always a small nation. History had been for them one
long disaster. It was clear to them that by human means they
would never reach the status they deserved as the chosen
people. So, bit by bit, they reached the conclusion that what

they could not achieve for themselves God must do; and they began to look forward to a day when God would intervene directly in history and raise them to the honour they dreamed of. The day of that intervention was *the day of the Lord*.

They divided all time into two ages. There was *the present age*, which was utterly evil and doomed to destruction; and there was *the age to come*, which would be the golden age of God. Between the two, there was to be *the day of the Lord*, which was to be the terrible first signs of the new age, often described in the same way as labour pains before a birth. It would come suddenly like a thief in the night; it would be a day when the world would be shaken to its very foundations; it would be a day of judgment and of terror. All over the prophetic books of the Old Testament and in much of the New Testament are descriptions of that day. Typical passages are Isaiah 2:12, 13:6ff.; Amos 5:18; Zephaniah 1:7; Joel 2; 1 Thessalonians 5:2ff.; 2 Peter 3:10.

Here, Peter is saying to the Jews: 'For generations, you have dreamed of the day of God, the day when God would break into history. Now, in Jesus, that day has come.' Behind all the old imagery stands the great truth that, in Jesus, God arrived in person on the scene of human history.

LORD AND CHRIST

Acts 2:22–36

> 'Men of Israel, listen to these words. Jesus of Nazareth, a man approved by God to you by deeds of power and wonders and signs, which God, among you, did through him, as you yourselves know – this man, delivered up by the fore-ordained knowledge and counsel of God, you took and crucified by the hand of wicked men. But

God raised him up and loosed the pains of death because it was impossible that he should be held subject by it. For David says in regard to him: "Always I foresaw the Lord before me, because he is at my right hand so that I should not be shaken. Because of this my heart has rejoiced and my tongue has exulted, and, furthermore, my flesh shall dwell in hope, because thou wilt not leave my soul in the land of the dead nor wilt thou suffer thy Holy One to see corruption. Thou hast made known to me the ways of life. Thou shalt make me full of joy with thy countenance." Brethren, I can speak to you freely about the patriarch David, that he is both dead and buried and his memorial is among us to this day. Thus he was a prophet; and because he knew that God had sworn an oath to him, that one of his descendants should sit upon his throne, he spoke with foresight about the resurrection of the Christ, that he would neither be left in the world of the dead nor would his flesh see corruption. This Jesus God raised up, and all of us are his witnesses. So then, when he had been exalted to the right hand of God, he received the promise of the Holy Spirit from the Father and poured out this which you see and hear. For David did not ascend up into heaven, and yet he says: "The Lord said to my Lord, sit upon my right hand until I make thine enemies thy footstool for thy feet." So then let all the house of Israel certainly know that God has made this Jesus whom you crucified Lord and Christ.'

HERE is a passage full of the essence of the thought of the early preachers.

(1) It insists that the cross was no accident. It belonged to the eternal plan of God (verse 23). Over and over again, Acts states this same thing (cf. 3:18, 4:28, 13:29). The thinking found in Acts safeguards us from two serious errors in our

understanding of the death of Jesus. (a) The cross is not a kind of emergency measure flung out by God when everything else had failed. It is part of God's very life. (b) We must never think that anything Jesus did changed the attitude of God to men and women. It was *by God* that Jesus was sent. We may put it in this way: the cross was a window in time allowing us to see the suffering love which is eternally in the heart of God.

(2) Acts insists that this in no way lessens the enormity of what those who crucified Jesus actually did. Every mention of the crucifixion in Acts is loaded with a feeling of shuddering horror (cf. Acts 2:23, 3:13, 4:10, 5:30). Apart from anything else, the crucifixion shows supremely how horrifyingly sin can behave.

(3) Acts is out to prove that the sufferings and death of Christ were the fulfilment of prophecy. The earliest preachers had to do that. To the Jews, the idea of a crucified Messiah was incredible. Their law said: 'anyone hung on a tree is under God's curse' (Deuteronomy 21:23). To orthodox Jews, the cross made it completely impossible that Jesus could be the Messiah. The early preachers answered: 'If you would only read your Scriptures in the right way, you would see that all was foretold.'

(4) Acts stresses the resurrection as the final proof that Jesus was indeed God's chosen one. Acts has been called the Gospel of the Resurrection. To the early Church, the resurrection was all-important. We must remember this: *without the resurrection, there would have been no Christian Church at all*. When the disciples preached the centrality of the resurrection, they were arguing from experience. After the cross, they were bewildered and broken; their dream had gone and their lives had been shattered. It was the resurrection which changed all that and turned them from cowards

into heroes. It is one of the tragedies of the Church that so often the preaching of the resurrection is confined to Easter time. Every Sunday is the Lord's Day, and every Lord's Day should be kept as resurrection day. In the eastern Church on Easter Day, when two people meet, one says: 'The Lord is risen' and the other answers: 'He is risen indeed!' Christians should never forget that they live and walk with a risen Lord.

SAVE YOURSELVES

Acts 2:37–41

> When they heard this, they were pierced to the heart, and they said to Peter and to the other apostles: 'Brethren, what are we to do?' Peter said to them: 'Repent, and let each of you be baptized in the name of Jesus Christ so that your sins may be forgiven; and you will receive the gift of the Holy Spirit, for this promise is to you and to your children and to all who are afar off, to all those whom the Lord your God invites.' With many other words he gave his witness and he urged them: 'Save yourselves from this crooked generation.' So they accepted his word and were baptized, and on that day there were added to them about 3,000 people.

THIS passage shows with crystal clarity the effect of the cross. When people realized just what they had done in crucifying Jesus, their hearts were broken. 'I,' said Jesus, 'when I am lifted up from the earth, will draw all people to myself' (John 12:32). Everyone has had a hand in that event. Once, a missionary told the story of Jesus in an Indian village. Afterwards, he showed the life of Christ in slides projected against the whitewashed wall of a house. When the cross appeared on the wall, one man rose from the audience and ran forward, crying: 'Come down from that cross, Son of God. I, not you, should be hanging there.' The cross, when we understand what happened there, must pierce our hearts.

That experience demands a reaction. 'Repent,' said Peter, 'first and foremost.' What does repentance mean? The word originally meant an *afterthought*. Often, a second thought shows that the first thought was wrong; and so the word came to mean *a change of mind*. But, if we are honest, a change of mind demands *a change of action*. Repentance must involve both change of mind and change of action. We may change our minds and come to see that our actions were wrong; but we may be so much in love with our old ways that we will not change them. We may change our ways but our minds remain the same, changing only because of fear or prudence. True repentance involves a change of mind *and* a change of action.

When repentance comes, something happens *to the past*. There is God's forgiveness for what lies behind. Let us be quite clear that the *consequences* of sins are not wiped out. Not even God can do that. When we sin, we may well do something to ourselves and to others which cannot be undone. Let us look at it this way. When we were young and had done something bad, there was an invisible barrier between us and our mother. But when we went and said we were sorry, the old relationship was restored, and everything was right between us again. Forgiveness does not abolish the consequences of what we have done, but it puts us right with God.

When repentance comes, something happens *for the future*. We receive *the gift of the Holy Spirit*, and in that power we can win battles we never thought to win and resist things which by ourselves we would have been powerless to resist.

THE CHARACTERISTICS OF THE CHURCH

Acts 2:42–7

> They persevered in listening to the apostles' teaching,
> in the fellowship, in the breaking of bread and in prayers.
> Awe was in every soul; and many signs and wonders were
> done by the apostles. All the believers were together,
> and they were in the habit of selling their goods and posses-
> sions and of distributing them among all as each had need.
> Daily they continued with one accord in the Temple,
> and breaking bread from house to house they received
> their food with joy and in sincerity of heart; and they
> kept praising God and everyone liked them. Daily the
> Lord added to them those who were being saved.

IN this passage, we have a kind of lightning summary of the
characteristics of the early Church.

(1) It was *a learning Church*; it persisted in listening to
the apostles as they taught. One of the great perils of the
Church is to look back instead of forward. Because the riches
of Christ are inexhaustible, we should always be going
forward. We should count it a wasted day when we do not
learn something new and when we have not penetrated more
deeply into the wisdom and the grace of God.

(2) It was *a Church of fellowship*; it had what someone
has called the great quality of *togetherness*. Admiral Nelson
explained one of his victories by saying: 'I had the happiness
to command a band of brothers.' The Church is a real Church
only when it has that kind of fellowship.

(3) It was *a praying Church*; these early Christians knew
that they could not meet life in their own strength and that
they did not need to. They always went in to God before they
went out to the world; they were able to meet the problems of
life because they had first met him.

(4) It was *a reverent Church*; in verse 43, the word which the Authorized Version correctly translates as *fear* has the idea of *awe* in it. It was said of a great Greek that he moved through this world as if it were a temple. Christians live in reverence because they know that the whole earth is the temple of the living God.

(5) It was *a Church where things happened*; signs and wonders were there (verse 43). If we expect great things from God and attempt great things for God, things happen. More things would happen if we believed that God and we together could make them happen.

(6) It was *a sharing Church* (verses 44–5); these early Christians had an intense feeling of responsibility for each other. It was said of William Morris, the nineteenth-century writer and artist, that he never saw a drunk man without having a feeling of personal responsibility for him. Real Christians cannot bear to have too much when others have too little.

(7) It was *a worshipping Church* (verse 46); they never forgot to visit God's house. We must remember that 'God knows nothing of solitary religion.' Things can happen when we come together. God's Spirit moves upon his worshipping people.

(8) It was *a happy Church* (verse 46); gladness was there. A gloomy Christian is a contradiction in terms.

(9) It was *a Church whose people others could not help liking*. There are two Greek words for *good*. *Agathos* simply describes a thing as good. *Kalos* means that a thing not only is good but also looks good; it has a charm and attractiveness about it. Real Christianity is a lovely thing. There are so many people who are good but who with their goodness possess a streak of unlovely hardness. J. P. Struthers, minister of the Reformed Presbyterian church in Greenock, used to say that it would help the Church more than anything else if Christians

would from time to time do a *bonnie thing*. In the early Church, there was a charm about God's people.

A NOTABLE DEED IS DONE

Acts 3:1–10

> Peter and John used to go up to the Temple at the hour of prayer at 3 pm; and a man who had been lame from the day of his birth was in the habit of being carried there. Every day, they used to put him at the gate of the Temple which is called the Beautiful Gate, so that he could beg for alms from the people who were going into the Temple. When he saw Peter and John about to go into the Temple, he asked to be given alms. Peter fixed his eyes on him with John and said: 'Look at us.' He paid attention to them because he was expecting to get something from them. Peter said to him: 'Silver and gold I do not possess, but what I have I give you. In the name of Jesus Christ of Nazareth – walk!' And he took him by the right hand and lifted him up. Immediately his feet and ankle bones were strengthened, and he leaped up and stood and walked about; and he went into the Temple with them, walking about and leaping and praising God. Everyone saw him walking about and praising God; and they recognized him as the man who had sat at the Beautiful Gate of the Temple to receive alms. They were filled with amazement and astonishment at what had happened to him.

THE Jewish day began at 6 am and ended at 6 pm. For devout Jews, there were three special times for prayer – morning, noon and evening. They agreed that prayer was effective wherever it was offered, but they felt that it was doubly precious when offered in the Temple courts. It is very interesting that the apostles kept up the customs in which they had been trained. It was the hour of prayer, and Peter and John were going into the Temple to observe it. A new faith had come to them, but they did not use that as an excuse to break the old law. They were aware that the new faith and the old discipline could walk hand in hand.

In the middle east, it was the custom for beggars to sit at the entrance to a temple or a shrine. Such a place was considered the best of all positions because, when people are on their way to worship God, they are disposed to be generous to others. W. H. Davies, the tramp poet, tells how one of his vagrant friends told him that, whenever he came into a new town, he looked for a church spire with a cross on the top and began to beg in that area. Love of other people and love of God must always go hand in hand.

This incident brings us face to face with the question of miracles in the apostolic times. There are certain definite things to be said.

(1) Such miracles *did* happen. In Acts 4:16, we read how the Sanhedrin knew that they must accept the miracle. The enemies of Christianity would have been the first to deny miracles if they could; but they never even try to deny them.

(2) Why did they stop? Certain suggestions have been made. (a) There was a time when miracles were necessary. In that period, they were needed as a guarantee of the truth and the power of the Christian message in its initial attack on the world. (b) At that time, two special circumstances came together. First, there were still those among the apostles who had had personal contact with Jesus Christ, which could never be repeated. Second, there was an atmosphere of expectancy when faith was in full flow. These two things combined to produce effects which were unique.

(3) The real question is not 'Why have miracles stopped?' but 'Have they stopped?' It is the simple fact that any doctor or surgeon can now do things which in apostolic times would have been regarded as miracles. God has revealed new truth and new knowledge to us, and through that revelation they are still performing miracles. As a great doctor said, 'I bandage the wounds; but God heals them.' For Christians, there are still miracles all around if they have eyes to see.

THE SHAME OF THE CROSS

Acts 3:11–16

> As he clung to Peter and John, everyone came running to them in the colonnade which is called Solomon's, in a state of complete astonishment. When Peter saw them, he said to them: 'Men of Israel, why are you surprised at this? Or why do you keep staring at us, as if we had made him walk by our own power or goodness? The God of Abraham and of Isaac and of Jacob, your fathers' God, has glorified his servant Jesus, whom you handed over and disowned before Pilate, when he had given judgment for his release. You disowned the holy and the just one and you asked for a man who was a murderer to be given to you as a favour. You killed the pioneer of life, but God raised him from the dead; and we are his witnesses. And his name, through faith in his name, has given strength to this man whom you see and know. It is the faith which is through him, which has thus given him back his health in presence of you all.'

HERE sound three of the dominant notes of early Christian preaching.

(1) The early preachers always stressed the basic fact that the crucifixion was the most shameful act in human history.

Whenever they speak of it, there is a kind of shocked horror in their voices. They tried to wound people's minds with the realization of the sheer enormity of what happened on the cross. It is as if they said: 'Look what sin can do.'

(2) The early preachers always stressed the vindication of the resurrection. It is the simple fact that without the resurrection the Church would never have come into being. The resurrection was proof that Jesus was indestructible and was Lord of life and of death. It was the final proof that behind him there was God and therefore a power which nothing could stop.

(3) The early preachers always stressed the power of the risen Lord. They never regarded themselves as the sources of power but only as channels of power. They were well aware of their limitations but were also well aware that there was no limitation to what the risen Christ could do through them and with them. Here lies the secret of the Christian life. As long as Christians think only of what *they* can do and be, there can be nothing but failure and frustration and fear. But when a Christian thinks of 'not I, but Christ in me', there can be nothing but peace and power.

THE NOTES OF PREACHING

Acts 3:17–26

'Now, brothers, I know that it was through ignorance that you did it, just as your rulers did. But God has thus fulfilled those things which he foretold by the mouths of all the prophets that his Anointed One should suffer. Repent, then, and turn so that your sins may be wiped out, so that times of refreshing may come to you from God, and so that he may send Jesus Christ who has already been preached to you. It is necessary that heaven

38

should receive him until the times when all things shall
be restored, times of which God spoke through the
mouths of his holy prophets since the world began.
Moses said: "The Lord, your God, will raise up from
your brethren a prophet like me. You must listen to him
in everything that he will say to you; and it will be that
everyone who will not listen to that prophet will be
utterly destroyed from the people." And all the prophets
who spoke from Samuel, and those who succeeded him,
also announced the tidings of these days. You are the
sons of the prophets and of the covenant which God
made with your fathers when he said: "In your seed all
the nations of the earth will be blessed." It is to you first
that God, when he raised up his son, sent him to bless
you by making each one of you turn away from your
evil deeds.'

ALMOST all the notes of early Christian preaching are sounded
in this short passage.

(1) It begins with a note of mercy and warning combined.
It was in ignorance that the Jews perpetrated the terrible deed
of the crucifixion; but that ignorance is no longer possible,
and, therefore, there can be no excuse for further rejection of
Jesus Christ. This note of the terrifying responsibility of
knowledge sounds all through the New Testament. 'If you
were blind, you would not have sin. But now that you say,
"We see", your sin remains' (John 9:41). 'If I had not come
and spoken to them, they would not have sin; but now they
have no excuse for their sin' (John 15:22). 'Anyone, then,
who knows the right thing to do and fails to do it, commits
sin' (James 4:17). To have seen the full light of the revelation
of God is the greatest of privileges, but it is also the most
terrible of responsibilities.

(2) The obligation this knowledge brings is the obligation
to repent and to turn. The two words go closely together.

Repent might simply mean to change one's mind; and it is an easier thing to change one's mind than to change one's life. But this change of mind is to result in turning away from the old way and making a new start.

(3) This repentance will have certain consequences. It will affect the *past*; sins will be *wiped out*. This is a vivid word. Ancient writing was upon papyrus, and the ink had no acid in it. It therefore did not bite into the papyrus like modern ink, but simply lay on top of it. To erase the writing, it was simply wiped away with a wet sponge; so God wipes out the sin of those who are forgiven. It will affect the *future*; it will bring refreshing times. Into life will come something which will be a strength in weakness and a rest in weariness.

(4) Peter goes on to speak of the coming again of Christ. Whatever else that doctrine means, it means that history is going somewhere.

(5) Peter insists that all that has happened has been foretold. The Jews refused to accept the idea of a chosen one of God who must suffer; but Peter insists that if they search their own Scriptures they will find it all there.

(6) Peter reminds them of their national privilege. In a very special sense, the Jews were God's chosen people.

(7) Finally, he lays down the inescapable truth that that very special privilege brings very special duty. It is the privilege not of special honour but of special service.

ARREST

Acts 4:1-4

> While they were speaking to the people, the priests, the superintendent of the Temple and the Sadducees came upon them. They were annoyed because they were

teaching the people, and proclaiming, through Jesus, the resurrection from the dead. So they laid hands upon them and put them under arrest until the next day, for by this time it was evening. But many who heard the word believed; and the number of the men was about 5,000.

THE healing of the lame man had taken place within a part of the Temple area which was continually crowded with people. The spotlight of publicity was inevitably focused upon the incident.

The Beautiful Gate was the gate which led from the Court of the Gentiles into the Court of the Women. The Court of the Gentiles was both the largest and the busiest of all the Temple Courts, for into it anyone of any nation could come as long as the ordinary laws of decency and decorum were observed. It was there that the money-changers had their booths and the sellers of sacrificial victims their stalls. Round the outer boundary of the Temple area ran two great colonnades meeting at a right angle in the corner of the Court of the Gentiles. One was the Royal Porch, the other Solomon's Porch. They, too, were crowded with people who had come to worship, to learn and to sightsee. Clearly, the whole series of events would gain the widest publicity.

Into this crowded scene came the priests, the superintendent of the Temple and the Sadducees. The man whom the Authorized Version calls the *captain* of the Temple was an official called the *sagan*. He was the high priest's right-hand man. In particular, he had the oversight of the good order of the Temple. When the crowd had gathered, it was inevitable that he and his Temple police should arrive on the scene. With him came the Sadducees, who were the wealthy, aristocratic class. There were not many of them, but they were rich and of great influence. The whole matter annoyed them very greatly for two reasons. First, they did not believe in resurrection from the dead; and it was this very truth that the apostles were proclaiming. Second, just because they were wealthy aristocrats, the Sadducean party was collaborationist. They tried to keep on friendly terms with the Romans in order that they might retain their wealth and comfort and status and power. The Roman government was very tolerant, but on public disorder it was merciless. The Sadducees were sure that, if the apostles were allowed to go on unchecked, riots and civil disorder might follow, with disastrous consequences to their status. Therefore they proposed to nip this movement in the bud; and that is why Peter and John were so promptly arrested. It is a terrible example of a party of individuals who, in order to retain their vested interests, would not listen to the truth themselves or give anyone else a chance to hear it.

BEFORE THE SANHEDRIN

Acts 4:5-12

So on the next day it happened that the rulers and the elders and the scribes were assembled in Jerusalem, together with Annas the high priest, and Caiaphas and John and Alexander and all those who belonged to the priestly families. So they set them in the midst and asked them: 'By what power or by what name have you done this?' Then Peter, filled with the Holy Spirit, said to them: 'Rulers of the people and elders, if today we are being examined about the good deed done to the infirm man, if you are asking us by what means he has been restored to health, let it be known to all of you and to all the peoples of Israel that it is by the name of Jesus Christ of Nazareth, whom you crucified and whom God raised from the dead – it is by this name that this man stands before you in sound health. This is the stone which was

set at naught by you builders, which has now become
the head of the corner; and in no other is there salvation;
for there is no other name under heaven, given among
men, by which we must be saved.'

THE court before which Peter and John were brought was the
Sanhedrin, the supreme court of the Jews. Even in Roman
times, it had the right to arrest people. The one thing it could
not do was to pass the death sentence, except in the single
case of a Gentile who trespassed on the inner courts of the
Temple.

The Sanhedrin had seventy-one members. The high priest
was president because of his position. In the Sanhedrin there
were priests, practically all of whom were Sadducees. Their
one desire was to preserve the status quo so that their own
benefits might not be lessened. There were scribes, who
were the experts in the traditional law. There were Pharisees,
who were fanatics for the law. There were elders, who were
respected in the community.

There were also those described as being of 'the priestly
families'; these are the same people who are sometimes called
chief priests. They consisted of two classes. First, there were
ex-high priests. In the great days, the high priesthood had
been hereditary and for life; but in the Roman times the office
was the subject of intrigue, bribery and corruption, and high
priests rose and fell, so that between 37 BC and AD 67 there
were no fewer than twenty-eight. But even after a high priest
had been deposed, he often remained the power behind the
throne. Second, although the high priesthood had ceased to
be hereditary, it was still the prerogative of a very few families.
Of the twenty-eight high priests already mentioned, all but
six came from four priestly families. The members of these
families had a special status, and it is they who were known
as the chief priests.

When we read Peter's speech, and remember to whom it was spoken, we recognize one of the world's great demonstrations of courage. It was spoken to an audience of the wealthiest, the most intellectual and the most powerful in the land – and yet Peter, the Galilaean fisherman, faces them rather as their judge than as their victim. Further, this was the very court which had condemned Jesus to death. Peter knew that he was taking his life in his hands.

There are two kinds of courage. There is the reckless courage, which is hardly aware of the dangers it is facing. There is the far higher, cool courage, which knows the peril in which it stands and refuses to be daunted. It was that second courage that Peter demonstrated. When Achilles, the great warrior of the Greeks, was told that if he went out to battle he would surely die, he answered in the immortal sentence: 'Nevertheless, I am for going on.' Peter, in that moment, knew the peril in which he stood; nevertheless, he, too, was for going on.

LOYALTY ONLY TO GOD

Acts 4:13–22

> When they saw how boldly Peter and John spoke, and when they had grasped the fact that they were men with no special knowledge and no special qualifications, they were amazed; and they recognized them for men who had been in the company of Jesus. So, as they looked at the man who was cured and who was standing with them, they could find no charge to make. They ordered them to leave the Sanhedrin, and they discussed with each other: 'What are we to do with these men? For, that, through them, a notable sign has happened is plain to all who live in Jerusalem, and we cannot deny it. But, in

44

order that this may not spread any further throughout the people, let us forbid them with threats to speak any more in this name to any man.' So they summoned them in and ordered them absolutely to abstain from teaching in the name of Jesus. But Peter and John said to them: 'You must judge whether, in the sight of God, it is right to listen to you rather than to God; for we are unable not to speak the things that we have seen and heard.' But they added still further threats and let them go because they could find no means of punishing them because of the people, for everyone glorified God at what had happened, for the man on whom the sign of healing had taken place was more than forty years old.

HERE we see very vividly both the enemy's attack and the Christian defence. In the enemy's attack, there are two characteristics. First, there is *contempt*. The Authorized Version says that the Sanhedrin regarded Peter and John as unlearned and ignorant men. The word translated as *unlearned* means that they had no kind of technical education, especially in the intricate regulations of the law. The word translated as *ignorant* means that they had no special professional qualifications. The Sanhedrin, as it were, regarded them as men without a college education and with no professional status. It is often difficult for ordinary people to deal with what might be called academic and professional snobbery. But those who have Christ in their hearts possess a real dignity which neither academic attainment nor professional status can give. Second, there are *threats*. But Christians know that anything the world does to them is only for a moment, whereas the things of God last forever.

Faced with this attack, Peter and John had certain defences. First, they had the defence of an *unanswerable fact*. That the man had been cured, it was impossible to deny. The most unanswerable defence of Christianity is the individual Christian. Second, they had the defence of an utter *loyalty to God*. If it was a question of choosing between obeying other people and obeying God, Peter and John were in no doubt as to what course to take. As the writer H. G. Wells said, 'The trouble with so many people is that the voice of their neighbours sounds louder in their ears than the voice of God.' The real secret of Christianity lies in that great tribute once paid to the Scottish reformer John Knox: 'He feared God so much that he never feared the face of any man.' But the third defence was greatest of all – the defence of a *personal experience of Jesus Christ*. Their message was not something that they had simply heard from others. They knew at first hand that it was true, and they were so sure of it that they were willing to stake their lives upon it.

THE TRIUMPHANT RETURN

Acts 4:23–31

> When they had been released, they came to their own people and they told them all that the chief priests and elders had said to them. When they had heard the story, with one accord, they lifted up their voice to God and said: 'O Sovereign Lord, thou who hast made the heaven and the earth and the sea and all that is in them, thou who didst say, through the Holy Spirit by the mouth of David, our father, thy servant: "Why did the nations rage and the people set their thoughts on empty things?" The kings of the earth stood around and the rulers assembled together against the Lord and against his Anointed One. For in truth in this city they were assembled against thy holy servant Jesus, whom thou didst anoint – Herod and Pontius Pilate, with the Gentiles and the peoples of Israel

– to do all the things which thy hand and thy purpose fore-ordained should be done. So now, O Lord, look upon their threats and grant to thy servants to speak thy word with boldness, whilst thou dost stretch out thy hand to heal and whilst signs and wonders happen through the name of thy holy servant Jesus.' And when they had prayed, the place in which they were assembled was shaken and they were all filled with the Holy Spirit and kept on speaking the word with boldness.

In this passage, we have the reaction of the Christian Church in the hour of danger. It might have been thought that, when Peter and John returned with their story, a deep depression would have fallen on the Church as they looked ahead to the troubles which were now bound to descend upon them. The one thing that never even struck them was to obey the Sanhedrin's command not to speak any more. Into their minds at that moment came certain great convictions, and into their lives came a tide of strength.

(1) They had the conviction of the *power of God*. With them was the one who was creator and sustainer of all things. Once, the papal envoy threatened the reformer Martin Luther with what would follow if he persisted in his course, and warned him that in the end he would be deserted by all his supporters. 'Where will you be then?' demanded the envoy. 'Then as now,' Luther answered, 'in the hands of God.' For Christians, those who are for us are always more than those who are against us.

(2) They had the conviction of the *futility of human rebellion*. The word translated as *rage* is used of the neighing of lively horses. They may trample and toss their heads; in the end, they will have to accept the discipline of the reins. People may make their defiant gestures against God; in the end, God must prevail.

(3) They set before themselves the *remembrance of Jesus*. They remembered how he suffered and how he triumphed; and in that memory they found their confidence, for it is enough for Jesus' disciples to be the same as their Lord.

(4) They *prayed* for courage. They did not pretend that they could face this in their own strength; they turned to a power that was not their own.

(5) The result was the *gift of the Spirit*. The promise was fulfilled; they were not left comfortless. So they found the courage and the strength they needed to witness when their witness might well mean their death.

ALL THINGS IN COMMON

Acts 4:32–7

> The heart and soul of the crowd who had believed was one; and no one used to say that any of his possessions was his own, but they had all things in common. And the apostles kept on bearing witness to the resurrection of the Lord Jesus with great power, and great grace was on them all. Nor was anyone in need among them, for all who were owners of lands and houses made a habit of selling them and of bringing the proceeds of what they sold and of placing them at the apostles' feet. It was distributed to each, just as a man needed.
>
> Joseph, whose surname was Barnabas, one of the apostles (the translation of the name is Son of Consolation), who was a Levite and a native of Cyprus, possessed a field, and he sold it and brought the price and laid it at the apostles' feet.

In this new paragraph, there is a sudden change which is typical of Christianity. Immediately before this, all things were moving in the most exalted atmosphere. There were great thoughts of God; there were prayers for the Holy Spirit; there were quotations from the Old Testament that were full of praise. Now, without warning, the narrative changes to the most practical things. However much these early Christians had their moments on the heights, they never forgot that some-one did not have enough and that everyone must help. Prayer was supremely important; the witness of words was supremely important; but the culmination was love of the Christian community.

Two things are to be noted about them. (1) They had an intense sense of *responsibility for each other*. (2) This awoke in them *a real desire to share all they had*. We must note one thing above all – this sharing was not the result of legislation; it was utterly spontaneous. It is not when the law compels us to share but when the heart moves us to share that society is really Christian.

TROUBLE IN THE CHURCH

Acts 5:1–11

> A man called Ananias, together with his wife Sapphira, sold a bit of ground he had, and surreptitiously kept back part of the price, and his wife knew about it. He brought some part of the price and laid it at the feet of the apostles. Peter said to him: 'Ananias, why has Satan filled your heart so that you have deceived the Holy Spirit and kept back part of the price of your ground? While it remained yours did it not remain your own, and after it had been sold was it not entirely at your disposal? Why did you put this business into your heart? It is not to men you have lied but to God.' As Ananias listened to these words, he collapsed and breathed his life out. Great awe came upon all who heard it. The

young men rose and bound him up and carried him out and buried him.

After an interval of about three hours, his wife came in and she was not aware of what had happened. Peter said to her: 'Tell me, did you sell the piece of ground for so much?' 'Yes,' she said, 'for so much.' Peter said to her: 'Why is it that you agreed to tempt the Spirit of the Lord? Look now, the feet of those who have buried your husband are at the door and they will carry you out.' Immediately, she collapsed at his feet and breathed her life out. When the young men came in, they found her dead and they carried her out and buried her beside her husband. And great awe came upon the whole Church and upon all who heard these things.

THIS is the most vivid story in the book of Acts. There is no need to make a miracle of it. But it does show us something of the atmosphere which prevailed in the early Church. It is on record that Edward I once blazed with anger at one of his courtiers, and the man dropped dead in sheer fear. This story shows two things about the early Church – the power of suggestion on human minds and the extraordinary respect in which the apostles were held. It was in that atmosphere that the rebuke of Peter acted as it did.

This is one of the stories which demonstrate the almost stubborn honesty of the Bible. It might well have been left out, because it shows that even in the early Church there were very imperfect Christians; but the Bible refuses to present an idealized picture of anything. Once, a court painter painted the portrait of Oliver Cromwell, the Lord Protector of England. Cromwell was disfigured by warts on his face. The painter, thinking to please the great man, omitted the disfiguring warts. When Cromwell saw the picture, he said: 'Take it away, and paint me warts and all.' It is one of the great virtues of the Bible that it shows us its heroes, warts and all.

There is a certain encouragement in this story, for it shows us that even in its greatest days the Church was a mixture of good and bad.

Peter insists that sin is sin against God. We do well to remember that, particularly in certain directions. (1) Failure in care and true application is sin against God. Everything, however humble it may be, that contributes to the health, the happiness and the welfare of humanity is work done for God. Antonio Stradivari, the great maker of violins, said: 'If my hand slacked, I should rob God.' That is a motto for us all to take. (2) Failure to use our talents is sin against God. God gave us such talents as we have; we hold them in stewardship for him; and we are responsible to him for the use we make of them. (3) Failure in truth is sin against God. When we slip into falsehood, it is sin against the guidance of the Spirit in our hearts.

THE ATTRACTION OF CHRISTIANITY

Acts 5:12–16

> Many signs and wonders were done among the people through the hands of the apostles; and they were all together in Solomon's colonnade. Of the others, no one dared to meddle with them. But the people held them in the highest esteem; nay more, crowds of men and women believed in the Lord and attached themselves to them. The result was that they brought the sick to the streets and laid them on beds and pallets, so that, when Peter came, even his shadow might fall on some of them; and a crowd assembled from the cities round about Jerusalem carrying the sick and those who were troubled by unclean spirits; and all of them were healed.

HERE is a cameo-like picture of what went on in the early Church. (1) It tells us where the Church met. Their meeting place was Solomon's colonnade, one of the two great colonnades which surrounded the Temple area. The early Christians were constant in their attendance at the House of God, seeking all the time to know God better and to draw upon his strength for life and living. (2) It tells us how the Church met. The early Christians assembled where everyone could see them. They knew what had happened to the apostles and what might well happen to them; but they were determined to show everyone whose they were and where they stood. (3) It tells us that the early Church was a supremely effective Church. Things happened. The days when the healing ministry of the Church was in the forefront of its work are past, although they may well return. But the Church still exists to make bad people good; and people will always throng to a Church where lives are changed.

This passage closes with a reference to those troubled by unclean spirits. The ancient people attributed all disease to the work of such spirits. The Egyptians, for instance, believed that the body could be divided into separate parts and that every part could be inhabited by an evil spirit. Often, they believed that these evil spirits were the spirits of wicked people who had departed this life but were still carrying on their malignant work.

ARREST AND TRIAL ONCE AGAIN

Acts 5:17–32

> But the high priest and his party (the local sect of the Sadducees) were filled with envy, and they laid hands on the apostles and put them under public arrest. But

through the night the angel of the Lord opened the doors of the prison and led them out and said: 'Go, stand in the Temple and tell the people all the words of this life.' When they heard this, they came into the Temple very early and began to teach. When the high priest and those with him arrived, they summoned the Sanhedrin and all the council of the sons of Israel; and they despatched messengers to the prison that they should be brought. When the officers arrived, they did not find them in the prison. When they returned, they brought news saying: 'We found the prison shut with all security, and the guards standing at the doors, but when we opened the doors we found no one inside.' When the superintendent of the Temple and the chief priests heard these words, they did not know what to make of them and could not understand what could have happened. But someone arrived and told them: 'Look now, the men you put in prison are standing in the Temple and teaching the people.' Then the superintendent of the Temple went away with his officers and fetched them, but he used no force, for they were afraid of the people in case they might be stoned. When they had fetched them, they stood them amid the Sanhedrin. The high priest questioned them: 'We laid the strongest injunctions on you not to teach in this name; and, look now, you have filled Jerusalem with your teaching and you are aiming at bringing on us guilt for the blood of this man.' Peter and the apostles answered: 'It is necessary to obey God rather than men. The God of our fathers raised up Jesus whom you got into your hands and hanged on a tree. God has exalted him as Prince and Saviour at his right hand, to give repentance to Israel and remission of sins, and we are witnesses of these things, as is the Holy Spirit, whom God gave to those who obey him.'

THE second arrest of the apostles was inevitable. The Sanhedrin had strictly ordered them to abstain from teaching in the name of Jesus, and they had publicly disregarded that command. That, to the Sanhedrin, was a doubly serious matter. These apostles were not only heretics, they were also potential disturbers of the peace. Palestine was always a volatile country; if this were not checked, it might well result in some kind of popular rising; and that was the last thing the priests and Sadducees wanted, because then Rome would intervene.

There is not necessarily a miracle in the release of Peter and John. The word *aggelos* has two meanings. It means an angel; but it is also the normal word for a messenger. Even if the release of the apostles had been brought about by human means, the agent of the release would still be the *aggelos* of the Lord.

In the narrative of the events after the release, we see vividly displayed the great characteristics of these early Christians.

(1) They had courage. The command to go straight back and preach in the Temple sounds to a prudent mind almost incredible. To obey that command was an act of almost reckless boldness. And yet they went.

(2) They had principles. And their ruling principle was that in all circumstances obedience to God must come first. They never asked: 'Is this course of action safe?' They asked: 'Is this what God wants me to do?'

(3) They had a clear idea of their function. They knew that they were witnesses for Christ. Witnesses are essentially people who speak from first-hand knowledge. They know from personal experience that what they say is true; and it is impossible to stop people like that, because it is impossible to stop the truth.

AN UNEXPECTED ALLY

Acts 5:33-42

When they heard this, they were torn with vexation and planned to destroy them. But a certain Pharisee called Gamaliel stood up in the Sanhedrin, a teacher of the law held in honour by all the people, and ordered that the men should be put out of the meeting for a short time. He said to them: 'Men of Israel, take heed to yourselves regarding these men and think what you are going to do with them. Before these days Theudas arose, saying that he was someone. Men to the number of about 400 attached themselves to him. He was destroyed, and all who were persuaded by him were dispersed and came to nothing. After him Judas the Galilaean arose, in the days when the census was taken, and he persuaded the people to follow him. He too perished, and all the people who were persuaded by him were scattered abroad. And in the present circumstances I say to you – keep off these men and let them go, because if this purpose and this affair is of men it will come to nothing; but if it is of God you cannot stop them. So take care that you do not turn out to be men who are fighting against God.' They were persuaded by him. So they called in the apostles, and, when they had threatened them, they enjoined them not to speak in the name of Jesus and sent them away. So they went out from the presence of the Sanhedrin rejoicing because they were deemed worthy to suffer dishonour for the name. Every day in the Temple and from house to house they never stopped teaching and proclaiming the good news that Jesus was God's Anointed One.

ON their second appearance before the Sanhedrin, the apostles found an unexpected helper. Gamaliel was a Pharisee. The

Sadducees were the wealthy collaborationists, who were always seeking to preserve their own status; but the Pharisees had no political ambitions. Their name literally means 'the separated ones', and they had separated themselves from ordinary life in order to devote themselves to keeping the law in every small detail. There were never more than about 6,000 of them in total, and the austerity of their lives made them highly respected.

Gamaliel was more than respected; he was loved. He was a kindly man with a far wider tolerance than his fellows. He was, for instance, one of the very few Pharisees who did not regard Greek culture as sinful. He was one of the very few to whom the title 'Rabban' had been given. He was called 'the Beauty of the Law'. When he died, it was said: 'Since Rabban Gamaliel died, there has been no more reverence for the law; and purity and abstinence died out at the same time.'

When the Sanhedrin seemed likely to resort to violent measures against the apostles, Gamaliel intervened. The Pharisees had a belief which combined fate and free will. They believed that all things were in the hand of God and yet that human beings were responsible for their actions. 'Everything is foreseen,' they said, 'yet freedom of choice is given.' So Gamaliel's point was that they must take care in case they were exercising their free will to go against God. He pleaded that, if this matter was not from God, it would come to nothing anyway. He quoted two examples.

First, he cited Theudas. In those days, Palestine had a quick succession of leaders who stirred up the people and set themselves up as the deliverers of their country and sometimes even claimed to be the Messiah. Who this Theudas was, we do not know. There was a Theudas some years later who led a group of people out to the Jordan with the promise that he could divide the waters and that they would walk over without getting wet, and whose rising was swiftly dealt with. Theudas was a common name, and no doubt this was just another troublemaker like all the others.

His second example was Judas. He had rebelled at the time of the census, taken by the governor Quirinius in AD 6 in order to arrange taxation. Judas took up the position that God was the King of Israel; tribute was due to him alone; all other taxation was without due reverence for God, and to pay it was a blasphemy. He attempted to raise a revolution but failed. The Sanhedrin listened to Gamaliel – and once again, after threatening the apostles, they let them go.

They went out rejoicing in their suffering. They rejoiced in persecution for two reasons. (1) It was an opportunity to demonstrate their loyalty to Christ. In Russia in the early days of communism, those who could show the marks of the fetters on their hands and the mark of the lash on their backs were held in honour because they had suffered for the cause. In John Bunyan's *The Pilgrim's Progress*, it was Mr Valiant-for-Truth's proud boast: 'My marks and scars I carry with me.' (2) It was a real opportunity to share in the experience of Christ. Those who shared in the cross-bearing would share in the crown-wearing.

THE FIRST OFFICE-BEARERS

Acts 6:1–7

In those days, when the number of the disciples was growing, there arose a complaint of the Greek-speaking Jews against the Hebrew-speaking Jews, in which they alleged that their widows were being overlooked in the daily distribution. The Twelve sent for the main body of the disciples and said: 'It is not fitting that we should abandon the word of God to serve tables. So, brethren,

look about for seven attested men from your number,
men full of the Holy Spirit and of wisdom, and we will
put them in charge of this business. As for us, we will
give our undivided attention to prayer and to the service
of the word.' This seemed a good idea to the body of
the disciples. So they chose Stephen, a man full of
faith and of the Holy Spirit, and Philip and Prochoros
and Nicanor and Timon and Parmenos and Nicolaos,
who was a Gentile from Antioch who had embraced
the Jewish faith. They brought these men into the
presence of the apostles, and they prayed and laid their
hands upon them. So the word of God progressed and
the number of disciples in Jerusalem was very greatly
increased; and a large number of the priests accepted
the faith.

As the Church grew, it began to encounter the problems of an
institution. The Jewish nation has always had a great sense of
responsibility for those who are less fortunate.

In the synagogue, there was a routine custom. Two collec-
tors went round the market and the private houses every Friday
morning and made a collection for the needy, partly in money
and partly in goods. Later in the day, this was distributed.
Those who were temporarily in need received enough to
enable them to carry on; and those who were permanently
unable to support themselves received enough for fourteen
meals, that is, enough for two meals a day for the week ahead.
The fund from which this distribution was made was called
the *Kuppah*, or basket. In addition to this, a house-to-house
collection was made daily for those whose needs were more
pressing. This was called the *Tamhui*, or tray.

It is clear that the Christian Church had taken over this
custom. But among the Jews themselves there was a rift. In
the Christian Church, there were two kinds of Jews. There

were the Jerusalem and the Palestinian Jews, who spoke
Aramaic, the descendant of the ancestral language, and prided
themselves that there was no foreign element in their lives.
There were also Jews from foreign countries who had come
up for Pentecost and made the great discovery of Christ. Many
of these had been away from Palestine for generations; they
had forgotten their Hebrew and spoke only Greek. The natural
consequence was that the spiritually snobbish Aramaic-
speaking Jews looked down on the foreign Jews. This contempt affected the daily distribution of alms, and there was a
complaint that the widows of the Greek-speaking Jews were
being – possibly deliberately – neglected. The apostles felt
they ought not to get themselves mixed up in a matter like
this; so the Seven were chosen to find a solution to the situation
and to put things right.

It is extremely interesting to note that the first office-bearers
to be appointed were chosen not to talk but for practical
service.

A CHAMPION OF FREEDOM ARISES

Acts 6:8–15

> Stephen, full of grace and power, performed great
> wonders and signs among the people. There arose in
> debate with Stephen certain members of the synagogue
> of the Libertines and of the Cyrenians and of the
> Alexandrians, and of those from Cilicia and Asia; and
> they could find no answer to his wisdom and to the Spirit
> with whose help he spoke. So they formed a plot to
> introduce certain men who alleged: 'We heard this man
> speak blasphemous words against Moses and against
> God.' So they agitated the people and the elders and the
> scribes, and they came upon Stephen and seized him

and brought him to the Sanhedrin. Then they introduced false witnesses who alleged: 'This man never
stops saying things against the holy place and against
the law; for we have heard him say that Jesus of Nazareth
will destroy this place and will alter the customs which
Moses handed down to us.' And when all those who sat
in the Sanhedrin gazed intently at him, they saw his face
looking as if it were the face of an angel.

THE Church's appointment of these seven men had far-
reaching consequences. In essence, the great struggle had
begun. The Jews always looked on themselves as the chosen
people; but they had interpreted *chosen* in the wrong way,
regarding themselves as chosen for special privilege and
believing that God had no use for any other nation. At their
worst, they declared that God had created the Gentiles to be
fuel for the fires of hell; at their mildest, they believed that
some day the Gentiles would become their servants. They
never dreamt that they were chosen for service to bring all
men and women into the same relationship with God as they
themselves enjoyed.

Here was the thin end of the wedge. This is not yet a
question of bringing in the Gentiles. It is Greek-speaking Jews
who are involved. But not one of the Seven has a Jewish name;
and one of them, Nicolaos, was a Gentile who had accepted
the Jewish faith. And Stephen had a vision of a world for
Christ. To the Jews, two things were especially precious –
the Temple, the only place where sacrifice could be offered
and God could be truly worshipped; and the law, which could
never be changed. Stephen, however, said that the Temple
must pass away, that the law was only a stage towards the
gospel and that Christianity must go out to the whole wide
world. No one could withstand his arguments, and so the Jews
resorted to force and Stephen was arrested. His career was to

be short; but he was the first to see that Christianity was not only for the Jews but was God's offer to all the world.

STEPHEN'S DEFENCE

WHEN the Lord Protector of England, Oliver Cromwell, was outlining the education he thought necessary for his son Richard, he said: 'I would have him know a little history.' It was to the lesson of history that Stephen appealed. Clearly believing that the best form of defence was attack, he took a bird's-eye view of the history of the Jewish people and cited certain truths as condemnation of his own nation.

(1) He saw that the people who played a really great part in the history of Israel were those who heard God's command, 'Leave . . . and go out,' and were not afraid to obey it. With that adventurous spirit, Stephen implicitly contrasted the spirit of the Jews of his own day, whose one desire was to keep things as they were and who regarded Jesus and his followers as dangerous innovators.

(2) He insisted that people had worshipped God long before there was ever a Temple. To the Jews, the Temple was the most sacred of all places. Stephen's insistence on the fact that God does not dwell exclusively in any temple made with hands was not to their liking.

(3) Stephen insisted that when the Jews crucified Jesus they were only taking to a natural conclusion a policy they had always followed; for all through the ages they had persecuted the prophets and abandoned the leaders whom God had raised up.

These were hard truths for people who believed themselves to be chosen by God, and it is little wonder that they were infuriated when they heard them. We must watch for these recurring themes as we study Stephen's defence.

THE MAN WHO ANSWERED GOD'S CALL

Acts 7:1–7

> The high priest said: 'Is this so?' And Stephen said:
> 'Men, brothers and fathers, listen to what I have to say.
> The God of glory appeared to Abraham our father when
> he was in Mesopotamia, before he lived in Charran. He
> said to him: "Get out from your country and from your
> kindred and come here to a land which I will show you."
> Then he came out from the land of the Chaldaeans and
> took up his residence in Charran. After the death of his
> father, he removed from there and took up his residence
> in this land where you now live. God did not give him
> an inheritance in it, not even enough to set his foot upon.
> But he did promise him that he would some day give it
> to him for a possession and to his descendants after him,
> although at that time he had no child. God spoke thus –
> that his descendants would be sojourners in an alien land,
> that they would make slaves of them and treat them badly
> for 400 years. As for the nations to which they will be
> slaves, God said: "I will judge them, and after these years
> have passed, they will come out and they will serve me
> in this place." '

As we have already seen, it was Stephen's method of defence
to take a panoramic view of Jewish history. It was not the
mere sequence of events which was in Stephen's mind. To
him, every person and event symbolized something. He began
with Abraham, for in the most literal way it was with him
that, for the Jews, history began. In him, Stephen sees three
things.

(1) Abraham was a man who answered God's summons.
As the writer to the Hebrews put it, Abraham left home without knowing where he was to go (Hebrews 11:8). He was a

man of adventurous spirit. Bishop Lesslie Newbigin of the Church of South India tells us that negotiations towards that union were often held up by people demanding to know just where a particular step might lead. In the end, someone had to say to these careful souls: 'Christians have no right to demand to know where they are going.' For Stephen, God's servants were those who obeyed God's command even when they had no idea what the consequences might be.

(2) Abraham was a man of faith. He did not know where he was going, but he believed that, under God's guidance, the best was yet to come. Even when he had no children and when, humanly speaking, it seemed impossible that he should ever have any, he believed that some day his descendants would inherit the land God had promised to them.

(3) Abraham was a man of hope. In the end, he never saw the promise entirely fulfilled – but he never doubted that it would be.

So Stephen presents the Jews with the picture of an adventurous life, always ready to answer God's summons in contrast to their desire to cling to the past.

DOWN INTO EGYPT

Acts 7:8–16

'So he gave him the covenant of which circumcision was the sign. So he begat Isaac and he circumcised him on the eighth day. And Isaac begat Jacob and Jacob begat the twelve patriarchs. The patriarchs were jealous of Joseph and sold him into Egypt; but God was with him and rescued him from all his troubles and gave him grace and wisdom before Pharaoh king of Egypt. So he made Joseph the ruler of Egypt and of his whole house. There came a famine upon the whole of Egypt and Canaan, and great affliction; and our fathers could not find food. But Jacob heard that there was corn in Egypt, and he despatched our fathers there on their first visit. On the second visit Joseph's brothers discovered who he was, and Joseph's family became known to Pharaoh. So Joseph sent and invited Jacob his father to come together with all his relations, in all seventy-five persons. So Jacob came down to Egypt; and he himself died there and so did our fathers. They were brought over to Sychem and they were laid in the tombs which Abraham had bought at the price of silver from the sons of Emmor in Sychem.'

THE picture of Abraham is followed by the picture of Joseph. The key to Joseph's life is summed up in his own saying in Genesis 50:20. At that time, his brothers were afraid that, after the death of Jacob, Joseph would take vengeance on them for what they had done to him. Joseph's answer was: 'Even though you intended to do harm to me, God intended it for good.' Joseph was the man for whom apparent disaster turned to triumph. Sold into Egypt as a slave, wrongfully imprisoned, forgotten by those he had helped, the day came when, in spite of it all, he became prime minister of Egypt. Stephen sums up the characteristics of Joseph in two words – *grace* and *wisdom*.

(1) *Grace* is a lovely word. At its simplest, it means beauty in the physical sense; then it comes to mean that beauty of character which everyone loves. Its nearest English equivalent is *charm*. There was about Joseph that charm which is always evident in the really good person. It would have been all too easy for him to become embittered. But he dealt faithfully with each duty as it emerged, serving with equal devotion as slave or as prime minister.

(2) There is no word more difficult to define than *wisdom*. It means so much more than mere cleverness. But the life of Joseph gives us the clue to its meaning. In essence, wisdom is the ability to see things as God sees them.

Once again, the contrast is there. The Jews were lost in the contemplation of their own past and imprisoned in the mazes of their own law. But Joseph welcomed each new task, even if it was a rebuff, and adopted God's view of life.

THE MAN WHO NEVER FORGOT HIS OWN PEOPLE

Acts 7:17–36

'When the time for the fulfilment of the promise which God had told to Abraham drew near, the people increased and multiplied in Egypt, until there arose another king in Egypt who had no knowledge of Joseph. He schemed against our race and treated our fathers badly by making them cast out their children so that they would not survive. At this point Moses was born, and he was very comely in God's sight. For three months he was nurtured in his father's house. When he was put out, Pharaoh's daughter took him up and she brought him up as her own son; and Moses was educated in all the lore of the Egyptians. He was mighty in his words and in his deeds. When he was forty years of age, the desire came into his heart to visit his brothers, the sons of Israel. He saw one of them being maltreated and went to his help; and he struck the Egyptian and exacted vengeance for the man who was being ill-treated. He thought that his brothers would understand that God was going to rescue them through him, but they did not understand. The next day, he came upon the scene as two of them were fighting. He tried to reconcile them and to make peace between them. "Men," he said, "you are brothers. Why do you injure each other?" But the one who was injuring his neighbour pushed him away and said: "Who made you a ruler or a judge over us? Do you intend to murder me in the way you murdered the Egyptian yesterday?" When Moses heard this, he fled and he became a sojourner in the land of Midian. There he begat two sons. When forty years had passed, when he was in the desert in the neighbourhood of Mount Sinai, an angel appeared to him in a flame of fire in a bush. When Moses saw it, he was astonished at the sight. When he approached to see what it was, the voice of the Lord came to him: "I am the God of your fathers, the God of Abraham and of Isaac and of Jacob." Moses was afraid and dared not look. But God said to him: "Take your shoes off your feet, for the place on which you are standing is holy ground. In truth I have seen the evil that is being done to my people in Egypt and I have heard their groaning. I have come down to rescue them. Come now – I will send you to Egypt." This Moses whom they rejected saying: "Who made you a ruler and judge over us?" – this very man God despatched as ruler and rescuer by the hand of the angel who appeared to him in the bush. He led them out after he had performed wonders and signs in Egypt and at the Red Sea and in the wilderness for forty years.'

NEXT upon the scene comes the figure of Moses. For the Jews, Moses was above all the man who answered God's command to go out. He was quite literally the man who gave up a kingdom to answer God's summons to be the leader of his people. Our Bible story has little to tell us of the early days of Moses; but the Jewish historians had much more to say. According to Josephus, Moses was so beautiful a child that, when he was being carried down the street in his nurse's arms, people stopped to look at him. He was so brilliant in his youth that he surpassed all others in the speed and the eagerness with which he learned. One day, Pharaoh's daughter took him to her father and asked him to make him his successor on the throne of Egypt. Pharaoh agreed. Then, the tale goes on, Pharaoh took his crown and for a joke placed it on the infant Moses' head; but the child snatched it off and threw it on the ground. One of the Egyptian wise men standing by said that this was a sign that if he was not killed at once this child was destined to bring disaster on the crown of Egypt. But Pharaoh's daughter snatched Moses into her arms and persuaded her father to take no notice of the warning. When Moses grew up, he became the greatest of Egyptian generals and led a victorious campaign in far-off Ethiopia, where he married the princess of the land.

In the light of that, we can see what Moses gave up. He actually gave up a kingdom in order to lead his people out into the desert on a great adventure for God. So, once again, Stephen is making the same point. The great individual is not the one who, like the Jews, is chained to the past and jealous of personal privileges, but the one who is ready to answer God's summons and leave the comfort and the contentment that might have been.

A DISOBEDIENT PEOPLE

Acts 7:37-53

'It was this man who said to the sons of Israel: "God will raise up a prophet from among your brothers, like me." It was this Moses who was in the gathering of the people in the wilderness, with the angel who spoke to him in Mount Sinai, and with your fathers. It was he who received the living oracles to give to you. But your fathers refused to be obedient to him. They rejected him. In their hearts, they turned back to Egypt. They said to Aaron: "Make us gods who will go before us, as for this man Moses we do not know what has happened to him." So in those days they made a calf and they sacrificed to the idol they had made and they found their joy in the works of their hands. And God turned and gave them over to the worship of the host of heaven; as it stands written in the Book of the Prophets: "Did you not bring me slain victims and sacrifices for forty years in the wilderness, O house of Israel? But now you have accepted the tabernacle of Moloch and the star of the god Remphan, the images you have made in order to worship them. I will take you away to live in the lands beyond Babylon." Our fathers possessed the tent of witness in the wilderness, as he who spoke instructed Moses to make it according to the pattern which he had seen. Your fathers received it from one generation to another, and brought it in with Joshua at the time when they were gaining possession of the lands of the nations whom God drove back from before your fathers, right up to the time of David. He found favour with God and he asked to be allowed to find a dwelling place for the God of Jacob. But it was Solomon who built a house for him. But the Most High does not dwell in houses made with hands. As the prophet says, "Heaven is my throne, earth is a footstool for my feet." "What kind of house will you build for me?" says the Lord, "or where is the place where I will rest? Has not my hand made all these things?" Stiff-necked, uncircumcised in hearts and ears, you have always opposed the Holy Spirit. As your fathers did, so do you. Which of the prophets did your fathers not persecute? And they killed those who told before-

hand the tidings of the coming of the Just One, whom
you betrayed and whose murderers you became – you
who received the law by the disposition of angels – and
who did not keep it.'

THE speech of Stephen begins to accelerate. All the time, by
implication, Stephen has been condemning the attitude of the
Jews; now that implicit condemnation becomes explicit. In
this closing section of his defence, Stephen has woven together
several strands of thought.

(1) He insists on the continued disobedience of the people.
In the days of Moses, they rebelled by making the golden
calf. In the time of Amos, their hearts went after Moloch and
the star gods. What is referred to as the Book of the Prophets
is what we call the Minor Prophets. The quotation is actually
from Amos 5:27; but Stephen quotes not from the Hebrew
version but the Greek.

(2) He insists that they have had the most amazing
privileges. They have had the succession of the prophets; the
tent of witness, so named because the tablets of the law were
kept in it; and the law which was given by angels.

These two things are to be put side by side – continuous
disobedience and continuous privilege. The more privileges
someone has, the greater the condemnation if that person takes
the wrong way. Stephen is insisting that the condemnation of
the Jewish nation is complete because, in spite of the fact that
they had every chance to know better, they continuously
rebelled against God.

(3) He insists that they have wrongly limited God. The
Temple, which should have become their greatest blessing,
was in fact their greatest curse; they had come to worship it
instead of worshipping God. They had ended up with a Jewish
God who lived in Jerusalem rather than a God of all people
whose dwelling was the whole universe.

(4) He insists that they have consistently persecuted the prophets and – the crowning charge – that they have murdered the Son of God. And Stephen does not excuse them on the plea of ignorance as Peter did. It is not ignorance but rebellious disobedience which made them commit that crime. There is anger in Stephen's closing words, but there is sorrow too. There is the anger that sees a people commit the most terrible of crimes; and there is the sorrow that sees a people who have refused the destiny that God offered them.

THE FIRST OF THE MARTYRS

Acts 7:54–8:1

> As they listened to this, their very hearts were torn with vexation and they gnashed their teeth at him. But he was full of the Holy Spirit, and he gazed steadfastly into heaven and saw the glory of God and Jesus standing at God's right hand. So he said: 'Look now, I see the heavens opened and the Son of Man standing at God's right hand.' They shouted with a great shout and held their ears and launched themselves at him in a body. They flung him outside the city and began to stone him. And the witnesses placed their garments at the feet of a young man called Saul. So they stoned Stephen as he called upon God and said: 'Lord Jesus, receive my spirit.' Kneeling down he cried with a loud voice: 'Lord, set not this sin to their charge.' And when he had said this, he fell asleep. And Saul fully agreed with his death.

A SPEECH like this could only have one outcome; Stephen had courted death, and death came. But Stephen did not see the faces distorted with rage. His gaze had gone beyond the present, and he saw Jesus standing at the right hand of God.

When he said this, it seemed to them only the greatest of blasphemies; and the penalty for blasphemy was stoning to death (Deuteronomy 13:6ff.). It is to be noted that this was not a legal trial. It was a lynching, because the Sanhedrin had no right to put anyone to death.

The method of stoning was as follows. The criminal was taken to a height and thrown down. The witnesses had to do the actual throwing down. If the criminal was killed by the fall, well and good; if not, great boulders were hurled down upon the person until death resulted.

There are in this scene certain notable things about Stephen. (1) We see the secret of his courage. Beyond all that the world could do to him, he saw awaiting him the welcome of his Lord. (2) We see Stephen following his Lord's example. As Jesus prayed for the forgiveness of his executioners (Luke 23:34), so did Stephen. When George Wishart, the sixteenth-century Scottish reformer, was to be executed, the executioner hesitated. Wishart came to him and kissed him. 'Lo,' he said, 'here is a token that I forgive thee.' Those who follow Christ the whole way will find strength to do things which it seems humanly impossible to do. (3) The dreadful turmoil finished in a strange peace. To Stephen came the peace which comes to those who have done the right thing even if the right thing kills them.

The first half of the first verse of chapter 8 goes with this section. Paul has entered on the scene under his original name – Saul. The man who was to become the apostle to the Gentiles thoroughly agreed with the execution of Stephen. But, as St Augustine said, 'The Church owes Paul to the prayer of Stephen.' However hard he tried, Saul could never forget the way in which Stephen had died. Even at this early point, the blood of the martyrs had begun to be the seed of the Church.

THE CHURCH REACHES OUT

CHAPTER 8 is an important chapter in the history of the Church. The Church began by being a purely Jewish institution. Acts 6 shows the first murmurings of the great debate about the acceptance of the Gentiles. Stephen had had a mind which went far beyond national boundaries. Chapter 8 shows the Church reaching out. Persecution scattered the Church abroad, and where they went they took their gospel. Into chapter 8 comes Philip, who, like Stephen, was one of the Seven and who is to be distinguished from the Philip who was one of the Twelve. First, Philip preached to the Samaritans. The Samaritans formed a natural bridge between Jews and Gentiles, for they were half-Jew and half-Gentile in their racial descent. Then comes the incident of the Ethiopian eunuch in which the gospel takes a step out to a still wider circle. As yet, the Church had no conception of a world mission; but, when we read this chapter in the light of what was soon to happen, we see the Church unconsciously but irresistibly being moved towards its destiny.

SAVAGING THE CHURCH

Acts 8:1-4

> At that time, a great persecution broke out against the Church in Jerusalem. They were all scattered abroad throughout the districts of Judaea and Samaria, except the apostles. Pious men carried Stephen away to bury him, and they mourned greatly over him. As for Saul, he ravaged the Church. He went into house after house and dragged out both men and women and put them under arrest.

THE death of Stephen was the signal for an outbreak of persecution which compelled the Christians to scatter and to seek safety in the remoter districts of the country. There are two especially interesting points in this short section.

(1) The apostles stood firm. Others might flee, but they braved whatever dangers might come; and they did this for two reasons. (a) They were men of courage. The novelist Joseph Conrad tells that, when he was a young sailor learning to steer a sailing-ship, a gale blew up. The older man who was teaching him gave him just one piece of advice: 'Keep her facing it. Always keep her facing it.' The apostles were determined to face whatever dangers threatened. (b) They were good men. Christians they might be, but there was something about them that won the respect of all. It is told that a slanderous accusation was once levelled against Plato. His answer was: 'I will live in such a way that all men will know that it is a lie.' The beauty and the power of the lives of the apostles was so impressive that, even at a time of persecution, the authorities hesitated to lay their hands upon them.

(2) Saul, as the Authorized Version says, 'made havoc' of the Church. The word used in the Greek denotes a brutal cruelty. It is used of a wild boar ravaging a vineyard and of a wild animal savaging a body. The contrast between the man who was savaging the Church in this chapter and the man who surrendered to Christ in the next is intensely dramatic.

IN SAMARIA

Acts 8:5-13

> Those who were scattered abroad went throughout the country telling the message of the good news. Philip

went down to the city of Samaria and preached Christ
to them. The crowds listened attentively to what Philip
had to say, as they heard his story and saw the signs
which he performed. Many of them had unclean spirits,
and the spirits, shouting loudly, came out of them; and
many who were paralysed and lame were cured; and
there was much rejoicing in that city.

A man called Simon was in the habit of practising
magic in the city and of bewildering the people of
Samaria. He alleged that he was someone great. Everyone, small and great alike, was greatly impressed by
him, for they said: 'This man is the power of God called
Great.' They were impressed by him because they had
been bewildered by his magical deeds for some considerable time. Both men and women were baptized
when they believed Philip, as he told them the good news
of the kingdom of God and of the name of Jesus Christ.
Even Simon himself believed, and, after he had been
baptized, he was constantly in Philip's company; and
he was amazed when he saw the signs and great deeds
of power which were happening.

WHEN the Christians were scattered far and wide, Philip,
who had emerged into prominence as one of the Seven, arrived
in Samaria; and there he preached. This incident of the
work in Samaria is an astonishing thing, because it was
widely acknowledged that the Jews had no dealings with the
Samaritans (John 4:9). The quarrel between the Jews and the
Samaritans was centuries old. Back in the eighth century BC,
the Assyrians conquered the Northern Kingdom, whose capital
was Samaria. As conquerors did in those days, they transported
the greater part of the population and settled strangers in the
land. In the sixth century, the Babylonians conquered the
Southern Kingdom with its capital at Jerusalem, and its
inhabitants were carried away to Babylon; but they completely

refused to lose their Jewish identity. In the fifth century BC, they were allowed to return and to rebuild their shattered city under Ezra and Nehemiah. In the meantime, those of the Northern Kingdom who had been left in Palestine had inter-married with the other races who had been brought in. When the people of the Southern Kingdom returned and started to rebuild their city, these people round Samaria offered their help. It was contemptuously refused because they were no longer pure Jews. From that day onwards, there was an unhealed rift and a bitter hatred between Jews and Samaritans.

The fact that Philip preached there and that the message of Jesus was given to these people shows the Church un-consciously taking one of the most important steps in history and discovering that Christ is for all the world. We know very little about Philip; but he was one of the architects of the Christian Church.

We must note what Christianity brought to these people. (1) It brought the story of Jesus, the message of the love of God in Jesus Christ. (2) It brought healing. Christianity has never been a matter of words only. (3) It brought, as a natural consequence, a joy that the Samaritans had never known before. It is a false Christianity which brings an atmosphere of gloom; true Christianity radiates joy.

THINGS WHICH CANNOT BE BOUGHT AND SOLD

Acts 8:14–25

> When the apostles in Jerusalem heard that Samaria had received the word of God, they despatched Peter and John to them. They came down and prayed for them, so that they might receive the Holy Spirit, for as yet the Holy Spirit had fallen on no one. It was in the name of

the Lord Jesus that they had been baptized. Then they laid their hands on them and they received the Holy Spirit. When Simon saw that the Holy Spirit was given through the laying on of the apostles' hands, he brought money to them and said: 'Give me too this power so that he on whom I lay my hands may receive the Holy Spirit.' Peter said to him: 'May your silver perish with you because you thought to obtain the gift of God for money; you have neither part nor lot in this matter, for your heart is not right before God. Repent of this wickedness of yours and pray God if it may be that the intention of your heart may be forgiven you. For I see that you are in the gall of bitterness and in the bond of wickedness.' Simon answered: 'Do you pray to the Lord for me, so that none of the things you spoke of may come upon me.'

So after they had borne their witness and spoken the word of God, they returned to Jerusalem, telling the good news to many villages of the Samaritans on the way.

SIMON was by no means unusual in the ancient world. There were many astrologers, fortune-tellers and magicians; and, in an age when people were easily taken in, they had a great influence and made a comfortable living. This is hardly surprising when even the twenty-first century has not risen above fortune-telling and astrology, as almost any popular newspaper or magazine can witness. It is not to be thought that Simon and his fellow practitioners were all conscious frauds. Many of them had deluded themselves before they deluded others, and believed in their own powers.

To understand what Simon was getting at, we have to understand something of the atmosphere and practice of the early Church. The coming of the Spirit upon an individual was connected with certain visible phenomena, in particular with the gift of speaking with tongues (cf. Acts 10:44–6). The person experienced an ecstasy which manifested itself in this strange phenomenon of uttering meaningless sounds. In Jewish practice, the laying on of hands was very common. With it, there was held to be a transference of certain qualities from one person to another. It is not to be thought that this represents an entirely materialistic view of the transference of the Spirit. The dominating factor was the character of the one who performed the laying on of hands. The apostles were held in such respect and even veneration that simply to feel the touch of their hands was a deeply spiritual experience. If a personal reminiscence may be allowed, I myself remember being taken to see a man who had been one of the Church's great scholars and saints. I was very young and he was very old. I was left with him for a moment or two, and in that time he laid his hands upon my head and blessed me. And throughout my life, I have continued to feel the thrill of that moment. In the early Church, the laying on of hands was like that.

Simon was impressed with the visible effects of the laying on of hands, and he tried to buy the ability to do what the apostles could do. Simon has left his name on the language, for *simony* still means the unworthy buying and selling of ecclesiastical positions and privileges. Simon had two faults.

(1) He was interested not so much in bringing the Holy Spirit to others as in the power and prestige it would bring to himself. This exaltation of self is a constant danger for preachers and teachers. It is true that they must take inspiration from being in the public eye; but it is also true – as the theologian James Denney said – that we cannot at one and the same time show that we are clever and that Christ is wonderful.

(2) Simon forgot that certain gifts are dependent on character; money cannot buy them. Again, preachers and teachers

must take warning. 'Preaching is truth through personality.' To bring the Spirit to others, it is not necessary to be wealthy; it is necessary to possess the Spirit.

CHRIST COMES TO AN ETHIOPIAN

Acts 8:26–40

The angel of the Lord spoke to Philip and said: 'Rise and go to the south by the road that goes down from Jerusalem to Gaza; that is Gaza in the desert.' So he arose and went. Now, look you, an Ethiopian eunuch, an influential official of Candace the queen of the Ethiopians, who was in charge of all her treasury and who had gone to worship in Jerusalem, was on his way home. As he sat in his chariot, he was reading the prophet Isaiah. The Spirit said to Philip: 'Go and join yourself to this chariot.' So Philip ran up and heard him reading the prophet Isaiah and said: 'Do you understand what you are reading?' He said: 'How could I do that unless someone were to guide me?' He invited Philip to get up and to sit with him. The passage of Scripture which he was reading was this – He was led as a sheep to the slaughter, and as a lamb before his shearer is dumb, so he did not open his mouth. In his humiliation he received no justice. Who will recount his lineage because his life is taken from the earth? The eunuch said to Philip: 'Tell me, please, who is the prophet speaking about? Is it about himself? Or about someone else?' Philip opened his mouth, and, taking his start from this passage of Scripture, told him the good news about Jesus. As they were going along the road, they came to some water. 'Look,' said the eunuch, 'here is water. What is to stop me being baptized?' And he ordered the chariot to stand still. So both Philip and the eunuch went down into the

water, and he baptized him. When they came up out of
the water, the Spirit of the Lord carried Philip away and
the eunuch no longer saw him, but he travelled along
his road rejoicing. Philip was found at Azotus. He went
through all the cities and preached the good news to
them until he came to Caesarea.

THERE was a road from Jerusalem which led via Bethlehem
and Hebron and joined the main road to Egypt just south of
Gaza. There were two Gazas. Gaza had been destroyed in a
war in 93 BC, and a new Gaza had been built to the south in 57
BC. The first was called Old or Desert Gaza to distinguish it
from the other. This road which led by Gaza would be one
where the traffic of half the world went by. Along came the
Ethiopian eunuch in his chariot. He was the chancellor of the
exchequer of Candace. Candace is not so much a proper name
as a title, the title which all the queens of Ethiopia bore. This
eunuch had been to Jerusalem to worship. In those days, the
world was full of people who were weary of the many gods
and the loose morals of the nations. They came to Judaism
and there found the one God and the austere moral standards
which gave life meaning. If they accepted Judaism and were
circumcised, they were called *proselytes*; if they did not go
that far but continued to attend the Jewish synagogues and to
read the Jewish Scriptures, they were called *God-fearers*. This
Ethiopian must have been one of these searchers who came
to rest in Judaism as either a proselyte or a God-fearer. He
was reading the fifty-third chapter of Isaiah; and, beginning
with that text, Philip showed him who Jesus was.

When he became a believer, he was baptized. It was by
baptism and circumcision that a Gentile entered the Jewish
faith. In New Testament times, baptism was largely adult
baptism. It was not that there was anything against infant
baptism; but, in those early days, men and women were

coming in from other faiths, and the Christian family had not had time to develop. To the early Christians, baptism was, whenever possible, by immersion and in running water. It symbolized three things. (1) It symbolized cleansing. As the body was cleansed by the water, so the soul was bathed in the grace of Christ. (2) It marked a clean break. We are told how one missionary, when he baptized his converts, made them enter the river by one bank and sent them out on the other, as if at the moment of baptism a line was drawn in their lives which sent them out to a new world. (3) Baptism was a real union with Christ. As the waters closed over an individual's head, that person seemed to die with Christ. The emergence from the water was seen as rising with Christ (cf. Romans 6:1–4).

Tradition has it that this eunuch went home and evangelized Ethiopia. We can at least be sure that, as he went on his way rejoicing, he would not be able to keep his new-found joy to himself.

SURRENDER

Acts 9:1–9

> But Saul, still breathing out threat and murder to the disciples of the Lord, went to the high priest and asked him for letters of credit to Damascus, to the synagogues there, so that if he found any of the Way there, both men and women, he might bring them bound to Jerusalem. As he journeyed, he came near Damascus. Suddenly a light from heaven flashed round about him. He fell on the ground and he heard a voice saying to him: 'Saul, Saul, why do you persecute me?' He said: 'Who are you, sir?' He said: 'I am Jesus whom you are persecuting. But rise; go into the city, and you will be

told what to do.' His fellow travellers stood speechless
in amazement, because they heard the voice but saw no
one. So Saul rose from the ground, but when his eyes
were opened he could see nothing. So they took him by
the hand and led him into Damascus. And for three days
he could not see, nor did he eat or drink anything.

Iɴ this passage, we have the most famous conversion story in
history. We must try as far as we can to enter into Paul's
mind. When we do, we will see that this is not a sudden conversion but a sudden surrender. Something about Stephen
lingered in Paul's mind and would not be banished. How could
a bad man die like that? In order to put his insistent doubt to
rest, Paul plunged into the most violent action possible. First,
he persecuted the Christians in Jerusalem. This only made
matters worse, because once again he had to ask himself
what secret these people had which made them face peril and
suffering and loss serene and unafraid. So, still driving himself
on, he went to the Sanhedrin.

The authority of the Sanhedrin extended wherever there
were Jews. Paul had heard that certain of the Christians had
escaped to Damascus, and he asked for letters of authority
that he might go to Damascus and order them to return. The
journey only made matters worse. It was about 140 miles from
Jerusalem to Damascus. The journey would be made on foot
and would take about a week. Paul's only companions were
the officers of the Sanhedrin, a kind of police force. Because
he was a Pharisee, he could have nothing to do with them; so
he walked alone; and as he walked he thought, because there
was nothing else to do.

The route went through Galilee, and Galilee brought Jesus
even more vividly to Paul's mind. The tension in his inner
being tightened. So he came near Damascus, one of the oldest
cities in the world. Just before Damascus, the road climbed

Mount Hermon, and below lay Damascus, a lovely white city in a green plain, 'a handful of pearls in a goblet of emerald'. That region had this characteristic phenomenon that when the hot air of the plain met the cold air of the mountain range, violent electrical storms resulted. Just at that moment came such a lightning storm, and out of the storm Christ spoke to Paul. In that moment, the long battle was over and Paul surrendered to Christ.

So he went into Damascus a changed man. And how changed! The one who had intended to enter Damascus like an avenging fury was led by the hand, blind and helpless.

There is all of Christianity in what the risen Christ said to Paul: 'Go into the city, and you will be told what to do.' Up to this moment, Paul had been doing what *he* liked, what *he* thought best, what *his* will dictated. From this time forward, he would be told what to do. Christians are men and women who have ceased to do what they want to do and who have begun to do what Christ wants them to do.

A CHRISTIAN WELCOME

Acts 9:10–18

> There was a disciple in Damascus called Ananias, and the Lord said to him in a vision: 'Ananias.' He said: 'Here am I, Lord.' The Lord said to him: 'Get up and go to the street called "Straight"; inquire in Judas' house for a man called Saul, a man from Tarsus. For, look you, he is praying; and he has seen a man called Ananias coming and putting his hands on him so that he may get back his sight.' Ananias answered: 'Lord, I have heard from many about this man. They have told me all the hurt he has done to the saints at Jerusalem. They have told me too how he has authority from the chief priests

to bind all who call upon your name.' The Lord said to him: 'Go, for he is a chosen instrument for my work. He is chosen to carry my name before peoples and kings and before the sons of Israel. I will tell him all he must suffer for my name's sake.' So Ananias went away and came to the house. He put his hands on him and said: 'Brother Saul, the Lord – Jesus who appeared to you in the way on which you were going – has sent me that you may get your sight back and so that you may be filled with the Holy Spirit.' Thereupon things like scales fell from his eyes and he got his sight back again. He rose and was baptized; and he took food and his strength increased.

WITHOUT a doubt, Ananias is one of the forgotten heroes of the Christian Church. If it is true that the Church owes Paul to the prayer of Stephen, it is also true that the Church owes Paul to the way in which Ananias treated him as a brother.

To Ananias came a message from God that he must go and help Paul; and he is directed to the street called 'Straight'. This was a major street that ran straight from the east to the west of Damascus. It was divided into three parts – a centre part where the traffic ran, and two side-walks where the pedestrians thronged and the merchants sat in their little booths and carried on their trade. When that message came to Ananias, it must have sounded insane to him. He might well have approached Paul with suspicion, as one doing an un-pleasant task; he might well have begun with recriminations; but no, his first words were: '*Brother Saul.*'

What a welcome! It is one of the most sublime examples of Christian love. That is what Christ can produce. The British evangelist Bryan Green tells that, after one of his campaigns in America in the 1960s, he asked at the last meeting that people should stand up and in a few words say just what the campaign had done for them. A girl stood up. Not a good speaker, she could only put a few sentences together, and this is what she said: 'Through this campaign I have found Christ and he made me able to forgive the man who murdered my father.' He made me able to forgive – that is the very essence of Christianity. In Christ, Paul and Ananias, who had been the bitterest enemies, came together as brothers.

WITNESSING FOR CHRIST

Acts 9:19–22

> Paul remained with the disciples in Damascus for some time. And immediately he began to preach Jesus in the synagogues, and the burden of his preaching was: 'This is the Son of God.' Everyone who heard him was astonished and kept saying: 'Is not this the man who at Jerusalem sacked those who call on this name? He came here too to bring them bound to the chief priests.' But Saul's power grew ever greater, and he confounded the Jews who lived in Damascus, by proving that this is God's Anointed One.

THIS is Luke's account of what happened to Paul after his conversion. If we want to have the chronology of the whole period in our minds, we must also read Paul's own account of the matter in Galatians 1:15–24. When we put the two accounts together, we find that the chain of events runs like this. (1) Saul is converted on the Damascus road. (2) He preaches in Damascus. (3) He goes away to Arabia (Galatians 1:17). (4) He returns and preaches in Damascus for a period of three years (Galatians 1:18). (5) He goes to Jerusalem. (6) He escapes from Jerusalem to Caesarea. (7) He returns to the

ACTS   9:23-5

regions of Syria and Cilicia (Galatians 1:21). So we see that
Paul began by doing two things.

(1) He immediately witnessed to his faith in Damascus.
In Damascus there were many Jews, and consequently there
would be many synagogues. It was in these Damascus
synagogues that Paul first lifted up his voice for Christ. That
was an act of the greatest moral courage. It was to these very
synagogues that Paul had received his letters of authority as
an official agent of the Jewish faith and of the Sanhedrin. It
would have been very much easier to begin his Christian
witness somewhere where he was not known and where his
past did not stand against him. Paul is saying: 'I am a changed
man and I am determined that those who know me best should
know it.' Already he is proclaiming: 'I am not ashamed of
the gospel of Christ.'

(2) The second thing he did is not mentioned by Luke at
all – he went to Arabia (Galatians 1:17). Into Paul's life had
come a shattering change, and for a time he had to be alone
with God. Before him stretched a different life, and he needed
two things: guidance for a way that was totally strange, and
strength for an almost overwhelming task that had been given
to him. He went to God for both.

ESCAPING BY THE SKIN
OF HIS TEETH

Acts 9:23-5

> After some time, the Jews formed a plot to murder him;
> but Saul was informed of their plot. Night and day they
> kept continuous watch on the gates to murder him. But
> the disciples took him by night and, by way of the wall,
> let him down in a basket.

THIS is a vivid example of how much a few words in the biblical narrative may imply. Luke says that *after some time* in Damascus these things happened. The period dismissed in that passing phrase was no less than three years (Galatians 1:18). For three years, Paul worked and preached in Damascus, and the Jews were so determined to kill him that they even set a guard on the gates in case he should escape. But the ancient cities were walled cities, and the walls were often wide enough for a chariot to be driven round the top of them. On these walls, there were houses whose windows often projected over the walls. In the dead of night, Paul was taken into one of these houses, let down with ropes in a basket and so smuggled out of Damascus and set on his way to Jerusalem. Paul is only at the gateway of his adventures for Christ, but even here he is escaping with his life by the skin of his teeth.

(1) This incident is a witness to Paul's courage. He must have seen the great gathering against him in the synagogues. He knew what had happened to Stephen, he knew what he had intended to do to the Christians and he knew what could happen to him. Clearly, Christianity for him was not going to be easy; but the whole tone of the incident shows to anyone who can read between the lines that Paul revelled in these dangers. They gave him a chance to demonstrate his new-found loyalty to that Master whom he had persecuted and whom now he loved.

(2) It is also a witness to the effectiveness of Paul's preaching. No one was able to argue against him; and the Jews, helpless in debate, resorted to violence. No one persecutes the person who is ineffective. The critic and playwright George Bernard Shaw once said that the biggest compliment you can pay an author is to burn his books. Someone else has said: 'A wolf will never attack a painted sheep.' False

Christianity is always safe; real Christianity is always in peril. To suffer persecution is to be paid the greatest of compliments because it is the certain proof that people think we really matter.

REJECTED IN JERUSALEM

Acts 9:26–31

> When he arrived in Jerusalem, he tried to make contact with the disciples. They were all afraid of him because they did not believe that he was a disciple. But Barnabas took him and brought him to the apostles and told them the story of how, upon the road, he had seen the Lord and that he had spoken with him, and that in Damascus he had spoken boldly in the name of Jesus. He went in and out with them in Jerusalem, speaking boldly in the name of the Lord. He talked and debated with the Greek-speaking Jews, but they tried to murder him. When the brethren got news of this, they took him down to Caesarea and sent him off to Tarsus.
>
> So the Church all over Judaea and Galilee and Samaria enjoyed peace as it was being built up; and, walking in the fear of the Lord and in the comfort of the Holy Spirit, it was constantly increased.

WHEN Paul arrived in Jerusalem, he found himself regarded with the gravest suspicion. How could it be otherwise? It was in that very city that he had ravaged the Church and had dragged men and women to prison. We have seen how, at crucial moments in his career, certain people were instrumental in winning Paul for the Church. First, the Church owed Paul to the prayer of Stephen. Then the Church owed Paul to the forgiving spirit of Ananias. Now we see the Church owing Paul to the big-hearted charity of Barnabas. When everyone else was steering clear of him, Barnabas took him by the hand and vouched for him.

By this action, Barnabas showed himself to be a true Christian.

(1) He was someone who insisted on believing the best of others. When others suspected Paul of being a spy, Barnabas insisted on believing that he was genuine. The world is largely divided into those who think the best of others and those who think the worst; and it is one of the curious facts of life that usually we see our own reflection in others and make them what we believe them to be. If we insist on regarding someone with suspicion, we will end by making that person act suspiciously. If we insist on believing in someone, we will end by compelling that person to justify that belief. As Paul himself said, 'Love thinks no evil.' No one believed in people as Jesus did – and it should be enough for Jesus' disciples that they imitate their Lord.

(2) He was someone who never held people's pasts against them. It is so often the case that, because people have made mistakes, they are forever condemned. It is the great characteristic of the heart of God that he has not held our past sins against us; and we should never condemn people because they once failed.

In this passage, we see Paul taking characteristic action; he debated with the Greek-speaking Jews. Stephen had been one of these Hellenists; and in all probability Paul went to the very synagogues where once he had opposed Stephen in order to witness to the fact that his life was changed.

Here again, we see Paul in peril of his life. For him, life had become a matter of hair's-breadth escapes. Out of Jerusalem, he was smuggled to Caesarea and from there to Tarsus. Once again, he is following the consistent policy of his life, for he goes back to his native city to tell them that

he is a changed man and that the one who changed him is
Jesus Christ.

THE ACTS OF PETER

Acts 9:32-43

In the course of a tour of the whole area, Peter came
down to the saints who lived at Lydda. There he
found a man called Aeneas who had been bedridden
for eight years. He was paralysed. So Peter said to
him: 'Aeneas, Jesus Christ heals you. Rise and make
your bed.' At once he stood up, and all who lived at
Lydda and at Sharon saw him, and they turned to the
Lord.

In Joppa there was a disciple called Tabitha – Dorcas
is the translation of her name. She was full of good works
and of deeds of charity which she never stopped doing.
It happened that at that time she fell ill and died. They
bathed her body and placed her in an upper room. Now
Lydda is near Joppa, and the disciples heard that Peter
was there. So they sent two men to him to invite him:
'Do not fail to come to us.' Peter rose and went with
them. When he had arrived, they took him to the upper
room. And all the widows stood by in tears, showing
him the coats and tunics that Dorcas used to make when
she was with them. Peter put them all out and knelt down
and prayed. He turned to her body and said: 'Tabitha,
rise.' She opened her eyes and she saw Peter and sat up.
He gave her his hand and raised her to her feet. He called
the saints and the widows and set her before them alive.
This event became known throughout the whole of
Joppa, and many believed on the Lord; and Peter
remained some time in Joppa, staying with a man Simon,
a tanner.

For a time, Paul has held the centre of the stage; but once again Peter takes the limelight. This passage really follows on from 8:25. It shows Peter in action. But it shows more than that. In the most definite way, it shows us the source of Peter's power. When Peter healed Aeneas, he did not say: '*I* heal you'; he said: 'Jesus Christ heals you.' Before he spoke to Tabitha – Tabitha is the Hebrew for a *gazelle*, and Dorcas is the Greek for the same word – Peter prayed. It was not his own power on which Peter called; it was the power of Jesus Christ. We think too much of what we can do and too little of what Christ can do through us.

There is one very interesting word in this passage. Twice the Christians at Lydda are called *saints* (verses 32 and 41). The same word is used earlier in the chapter by Ananias to describe the Christians at Jerusalem (verse 13). This is the word that Paul always uses to describe the church members, for he always writes his letters to the saints who are at such and such a place.

The Greek word is *hagios*, and it has far-reaching associations. It is sometimes translated as *holy*; but the root meaning of it is *different*. Basically, Christians are men and women who are *different* from those who are merely people of the world. But where does that difference lie? *Hagios* was particularly used of the people of Israel. They are specifically a *holy* people, a *different* people. Their difference lay in the fact that, of all nations, God had chosen them to do his work. Israel failed in its destiny. It was disobedient, and by its actions it lost its privileges. The *Church* became the true Israel; and the Christians became the people who are *different*, their difference lying in the fact that they were chosen for the special purposes of God.

So we who are Christians are not different from others in that we are chosen for greater honour on this earth; we are different in that we are chosen for a greater service. We are saved to serve.

A DEVOUT SOLDIER

Acts 10:1-8

> There was a man in Caesarea called Cornelius. He was a centurion in the battalion called the Italian battalion. He was a devout man and a God-fearer with all his household. He did many an act of charity to the people, and he was constant in prayer to God. About 3 pm in a vision, he clearly saw the angel of God coming to him and saying: 'Cornelius.' He gazed at him and he was awe-stricken. He said: 'What is it, sir?' He said to him: 'Your prayers and your works of mercy have gone up to God for a memorial; so now, send men to Joppa, and send for a man called Simon who is also called Peter. He is lodging with one Simon, a tanner, whose house is on the seashore.' When the angel who was speaking to him went away, he called two of his servants and a devout soldier who was one of his orderlies. He told them everything and despatched them to Joppa.

THE tenth chapter of Acts tells a story that is one of the great turning points in the history of the Church. For the first time, a Gentile is to be admitted into its fellowship. Since Cornelius is so important in Church history, let us gather together what we can learn about him.

(1) Cornelius was a Roman centurion stationed at Caesarea, the headquarters of the government of Palestine. The word which we have translated as *battalion* is the Greek word for a cohort. In the Roman military set-up, there was first of all the *legion*. It was a force of 6,000 men and therefore

was roughly equal to a division. In every legion, there were ten *cohorts*. A cohort therefore had 600 men and comes near to being the equivalent of a battalion. The cohort was divided into *centuries*, and over each century there was a *centurion*. The century is therefore roughly the equivalent of a company. The parallel to the centurion in the British military organization is a company sergeant-major. These centurions were the backbone of the Roman army. One historian of the period describes the qualifications of the centurion like this: 'Centurions are desired not to be overbold and reckless so much as good leaders, of steady and prudent mind, not prone to take the offensive to start fighting wantonly, but able when overwhelmed and hard-pressed to stand fast and die at their posts.' Cornelius, therefore, was a man who first and foremost knew what courage and loyalty were.

(2) Cornelius was a *God-fearer*. In New Testament times, this had become almost a technical term for Gentiles who, weary of the gods and the immoralities and the frustration of their ancestral faiths, had attached themselves to the Jewish religion. They did not accept circumcision and the law, but they attended the synagogue and they believed in one God and in the pure ethic of Jewish religion. Cornelius, then, was a man who was seeking after God; and, as he sought God, God found him.

(3) Cornelius was a man given to charitable acts; he was characteristically kind. His search for God had made him love other people; and those who love others are not far from the kingdom.

(4) Cornelius was a man of prayer. Perhaps as yet he did not clearly know the God to whom he prayed; but, according to the understanding that he had, he lived close to God.

PETER LEARNS A LESSON

Acts 10:9–16

> On the next day, when they were on the way and when
> they were getting near the city, about midday Peter went
> up to the housetop to pray. He became hungry and he
> wanted something to eat. When they were preparing the
> meal, a trance came upon him. He saw the heavens
> opened and he saw a kind of vessel coming down. It
> was like a great sheet and it was let down by the four
> corners to the earth. On it there were all four-footed
> animals, all animals that creep on the earth and all that
> fly in the air. A voice came to him: 'Rise, Peter, kill and
> eat.' But Peter said: 'By no means, Lord, because I have
> never eaten anything common or unclean.' And the voice
> spoke again the second time: 'What God has cleansed,
> do not you reckon common or unclean.' This happened
> three times; and thereupon the sheet was taken up into
> heaven.

BEFORE Cornelius could be welcomed into the Church, Peter
had to learn a lesson. Strict Jews believed that God had no
use for the Gentiles. Sometimes they even went as far as saying
that help must not be given to a Gentile woman in childbirth,
because that would only bring another Gentile into the world.
Peter had to unlearn that before Cornelius could be allowed
in.

There is one point which shows that Peter was already on
the way to unlearning some of the rigidness in which he had
been brought up. He was staying with a man called Simon,
who was a tanner (9:43, 10:5). A tanner worked with the dead
bodies of animals, and therefore was permanently unclean
(Numbers 19:11–13). No strict Jew would have dreamt of
accepting hospitality from a tanner. It was his uncleanness

that made it necessary for Simon to live on the seashore outside the city. No doubt this tanner was a Christian, and Peter had begun to see that Christianity abolished these unimportant laws and taboos.

At midday, Peter went to the roof to pray. The roofs of the houses were flat, and, since the houses were small and crowded, people often went up to the roof for privacy. There he had a vision of a great sheet being let down. Perhaps above the flat roof there stretched an awning to ward off the heat of the sun; and maybe in Peter's trance the awning became the great sheet. The word for *sheet* is the same as for a ship's *sail*. Maybe on the roof Peter was looking out on the blue waters of the Mediterranean and saw the ships' sails in the distance, and they wove themselves into his vision.

In any event, the sheet with the animals on it appeared to him, and the voice told him to kill and eat. Now the Jews had strict food laws, recorded in Leviticus 11. Generally speaking, the Jews could eat only animals which chewed the cud and whose hooves were cloven. All others were *unclean* and forbidden. Peter was shocked, and protested that he had never eaten anything that was unclean. The voice told him not to call what God had cleansed unclean. This happened three times so that there could be no possible mistake or dodging of the lesson. Once, Peter would have called a Gentile unclean; but now God has prepared him for the visitors who would come.

THE MEETING OF PETER AND CORNELIUS

Acts 10:17–33

> When Peter was at a loss in his own mind to know what this vision could mean, look you, the men who had been

sent by Cornelius had asked their way to Simon's house and stood at the door. They spoke and asked if Simon who was also called Peter was lodging there. When Peter was still thinking about the vision, the Spirit said to him: 'Look you, three men are looking for you. Rise and go down and go with them without any hesitation, because it is I who sent them.' So Peter came down to the men and said: 'Look you, I am the man you are looking for. Why have you come?' They said: 'Cornelius, the centurion, a good man and a God-fearer, one to whose worth the whole nation of the Jews bears witness, was instructed by a holy angel to send for you to come to his house and to listen to the words you would give him.' So he asked them in and gave them hospitality.

On the next day he rose and went with them, and some of the brethren from Joppa came with him. On the next day they came to Caesarea. Cornelius was expecting them and had invited along his kinsmen and his closest friends. When Peter was going to come in, Cornelius met him and fell at his feet and worshipped him. Peter raised him up and said: 'Rise; I, too, am a man.' So he went in, talking with him as he went. He found many who had assembled there, and he said: 'You know that it is against the law for a man who is a Jew to have contact with or to visit one of another race. But God has shown me not to call any man common or unclean. So I came without any objection when you sent for me.' So Cornelius said: 'Four days ago from this time, I was praying in my house at 3 pm, and, look you, a man stood before me in shining clothes and said: "Cornelius, your prayer has been heard and your deeds of charity have been remembered before God. Send therefore to Joppa and send for Simon who is also called Peter. He is lodging in the house of Simon, a tanner, on the seashore." Immediately I sent to you; and I am most

grateful that you have come. Now then, we are all
present before God to hear all that God has enjoined
you to tell.'

In this passage, the most surprising things are happening. Once
again, let us remember that the Jews believed that other nations
were quite outside the mercy of God. A really strict Jew would
have no contact with a Gentile or even with a Jew who did
not observe the law. In particular, strict Jews would never
have as a guest nor ever be the guest of someone who did not
observe the law. Remembering that, see what Peter did. When
the messengers of Cornelius were at the door – and, knowing
the Jewish viewpoint, they came no further than the door –
Peter asked them in and gave them hospitality (verse 23).
When Peter arrived at Caesarea, Cornelius met him at the
door, no doubt wondering if Peter would cross his threshold
at all – and Peter came in (verse 27). In the most amazing
way, the barriers are beginning to go down.

That is typical of the work of Christ. A missionary tells
how he once officiated at a communion service in Africa.
Beside him as an elder sat an old chief of the Ngoni called
Manly-heart. The old chief could remember the days when
the young warriors of the Ngoni had left behind them a trail
of burned and devastated towns and had come home with
their spears red with blood and with the women of their
enemies as booty. And what were the tribes which in those
days they had ravaged? They were the Senga and the
Tumbuka. And who were sitting at that communion service
now? Ngoni, Senga and Tumbuka were sitting side by side,
their hatred forgotten in the love of Jesus Christ. In the
first days, it was characteristic of Christianity that it broke
the barriers down; and it can still do that when given the
chance.

THE HEART OF THE GOSPEL

Acts 10:34–43

> So Peter opened his mouth and said: 'In truth I have
> come to understand that God has no favourites; but that
> in every nation he who fears him and acts righteously is
> acceptable to him. As for the word which God sent to
> the sons of Israel, telling the good news of peace through
> Jesus Christ – this is he who is Lord of all – you all
> know the affair that happened all over Judaea, after the
> baptism which John preached – you know about Jesus
> of Nazareth, about how God anointed him with the Spirit
> and with power, about how he went about healing all
> who were under the sway of the devil because God was
> with him; we are witnesses of all he did in the country
> of the Jews and in Jerusalem. And they took him and
> hanged him on a tree. It was he whom God raised up on
> the third day and made him evident, not to all the people
> but to the witnesses elected beforehand by God, to us
> who were with him and who ate with him and drank
> with him after he rose from the dead. And he gave us
> orders to preach to the people and to testify that this is
> he who was set apart by God, to be the judge of the
> living and the dead. To him all the prophets testify –
> that everyone who believes in him receives forgiveness
> of sins through his name.'

It is clear that we have here only the barest summary of what
Peter said to Cornelius, which makes it all the more important
because it gives us the very essence of the first preaching
about Jesus.

(1) Jesus was sent by God and equipped by him with the
Spirit and with power. Jesus, therefore, is God's gift to us.
Often, we make the mistake of thinking in terms of an angry
God who had to be pacified by something a gentle Jesus did.

The early preachers never preached that. To them, the very coming of Jesus was due to the love of God.

(2) Jesus exercised a ministry of healing. It was his great desire to banish pain and sorrow from the world.

(3) They crucified him. Once again, for those who can read between the lines, the sheer horror in the crucifixion is stressed. That is what human sin can do.

(4) He rose again. The power which was in Jesus was not to be defeated. It could conquer the worst that people could do, and in the end it could conquer death.

(5) Christian preachers and teachers are witnesses of the resurrection. To them, Jesus is not a figure in a book or about whom they have heard. He is a living presence whom they have met.

(6) The result of all this is forgiveness of sins and a new relationship with God. Through Jesus, the friendship which should always have existed between men and women and God, but which sin interrupted, has dawned upon the world.

THE ENTRY OF THE GENTILES

Acts 10:44–8

> When Peter was still saying these things, the Holy Spirit fell upon those who were listening to his word. All the Jewish believers who had come with Peter were amazed that the gift of the Spirit had been poured out on the Gentiles too, for they heard them speaking with tongues and magnifying God. Then Peter said: 'Can anyone stop water being brought? Can anyone stop those who have received the Holy Spirit, as we too received him, from being baptized?' And he ordered them to be baptized in the name of Jesus. Then they asked him to wait with them for some days.

EVEN as Peter was speaking, things began to happen against which even the Jewish Christians could not argue; the Spirit came upon Cornelius and his friends. They were lifted out of themselves in an ecstasy and began to speak with tongues. This, to the Jews, was the final proof of the astonishing fact that God had given his Spirit to the Gentiles too.

There are two incidental points of interest in this passage.

(1) As is always the case in Acts, these Gentile converts were baptized there and then. In Acts, there is no trace of one set of people only being able to administer baptism. The great truth was that it was the Christian Church which was receiving these converts. We would do well to remember that in baptism today it is not the minister who is receiving a child; it is the *Church* which is receiving the child on behalf of Jesus Christ and accepting responsibility for that child.

(2) The very last phrase is significant. They asked Peter to wait with them for some days. Why? Surely in order that he might teach them more. Our entry into church membership is not so much the end of the road as the beginning.

PETER ON HIS DEFENCE

Acts 11:1-10

The apostles and the brethren who were throughout Judaea heard that the Gentiles too had received the word of God. So when Peter came up to Jerusalem, those of the circumcision criticized him because, they said, 'You went in to men who had never been circumcised and you ate with them.' So Peter began at the beginning and told them the whole story. He said: 'I was praying in the city of Joppa; in a trance I saw a vision. I saw a kind of vessel coming down like a great sheet let

99

down by the four corners from heaven; and it came
right down to me. I was gazing at it and trying to make
out what it was and I saw on it the four-footed beasts
of the earth and the wild beasts and the creeping
animals and the animals that fly in the air. And I
heard a voice saying to me: "Rise, Peter, kill and eat."
I said: "By no means, Lord, because food which is
common or unclean has never entered my mouth."
Again the voice spoke from heaven: "What God has
cleansed, do not you reckon as common." This happened
three times; and they were all drawn up into heaven
again.'

THE importance that Luke attached to this incident is shown
by the amount of space he devoted to it. In ancient times, a
writer had by no means unlimited space. The book form had
not come into use. Writers used rolls of a material called
papyrus, which was the forerunner of paper and was made of
the pith of the papyrus plant, a kind of bulrush. Now a roll is
an unwieldy thing, and the longest roll that was used was
about thirty-five feet long, which would be almost precisely
the length required to hold the book of Acts. Into that space,
Luke had almost endless material to fit. He must have selected
with the greatest care what he was going to set down; and yet
he finds the story of Peter and Cornelius of such importance
that he twice relates it in full.

Luke was right. We usually do not realize how near
Christianity was to becoming only another kind of Judaism.
All the first Christians were Jews, and the whole tradition
and outlook of Judaism would have moved them to keep this
new wonder to themselves and to believe that God could not
possibly have meant it for the Gentiles. Luke sees this incident
as a notable milestone on the road along which the Church
was feeling its way to the idea of a world for Christ.

A CONVINCING STORY

Acts 11:11-18

'And, look you, thereupon, three men, who had been sent to me from Caesarea, stood at the house where we were. The Spirit told me to go with them and to make no distinctions. These six brethren also came with me and we came to the man's house. He told us how in the house he had seen the angel standing and saying: "Send to Joppa and send for Simon, who is also called Peter, who will speak words to you by which you and all your house will be saved." As I was beginning to speak, the Holy Spirit fell upon them, just as in the beginning he did upon you. And I remembered the Lord's word and how he said: "John baptized you with water, but you will be baptized with the Holy Spirit." If God gave the same gift to them as to us who have believed in the Lord Jesus Christ, who was I to be able to hinder God?' When they heard this, they had no protests to make and they glorified God, saying: 'So God has given life-giving repentance to the Gentiles too.'

THE fault for which Peter was initially on trial was that he had eaten with Gentiles (verse 3). By this action, Peter had outraged the ancestral law and traditions of his people. Peter's defence was not an argument; it was a statement of the facts. Whatever his critics might say, the Holy Spirit had come upon these Gentiles in the most notable way. In verse 12, there is a significant additional point. Peter says that he took six brethren with him. Together with himself, that made seven persons present. In Egyptian law, which the Jews would know well, seven witnesses were necessary to prove a case completely. In Roman law, which they would also know well, seven seals were necessary to authenticate a really important document.

So Peter is in effect saying: 'I am not arguing with you. I am telling you the facts, and of these facts there are seven witnesses. The case is proved.'

The proof of Christianity always lies in facts. It is doubtful if anyone has ever been argued into Christianity by verbal proofs and logical demonstrations. The proof of Christianity is that it works, that it does change people, that it does make bad people good, that it does bring the Spirit of God to men and women. It is when our deeds give the lie to our words that the gravest discredit is brought on Christianity; it is when our words are guaranteed by our deeds that the world is presented with an argument for Christianity which cannot be denied.

GREAT THINGS IN ANTIOCH

Acts 11:19–21

> Those who had been dispersed by the persecution following upon the death of Stephen went through the country as far as Phoenicia and Cyprus and Antioch, but they spoke the word to no one except to Jews. But some of them, men from Cyprus and Cyrene, came to Antioch and spoke to the Greeks too and told them the good news of the Lord Jesus. The Lord's hand was with them; and a great number believed and turned to the Lord.

IN restrained sentences, these few words tell of one of the greatest events in history. Now, for the first time, the gospel is deliberately preached to the Gentiles. Everything has been working up to this. There have been three steps on the ladder. First, Philip preached to the Samaritans; but the Samaritans after all were half-Jewish and formed, as it were, a bridge between the Jewish and the Gentile world. Second, Peter accepted Cornelius; but it was Cornelius who took the initiative. It was not the Christian Church that sought out Cornelius; it was Cornelius who sought out the Christian Church. Further, it is stressed that Cornelius was a God-fearer and, therefore, on the fringes of the Jewish faith. Third, in Antioch the Church did not go to people who were Jews or half-Jews, nor wait to be approached by Gentiles seeking admission; with determination and without waiting for the invitation, it preached the gospel to the Gentiles. Christianity is finally launched on its worldwide mission.

Here we have a truly amazing thing. The Church has taken the most epoch-making of all steps; and we do not even know the names of the people who took that step. All we know is that they came from Cyprus and Cyrene. They go down in history as nameless pioneers of Christ. It has always been one of the tragedies of the Church that people have wanted to be noticed and named when they did something worth while. What the Church has always needed, perhaps more than anything else, is people who never care who gains the credit for it as long as the work is done. These Christians may not have written their names in the history books; but they have written them forever in God's Book of Life.

Another striking feature is that this incident begins a section of Acts where Antioch occupies the centre of the stage. Antioch was the third greatest city in the world next to Rome and Alexandria. It stood near the mouth of the River Orontes, fifteen miles from the Mediterranean Sea. It was lovely and cosmopolitan, but it was notorious for luxurious immorality. It was famous for chariot-racing and for a kind of deliberate pursuit of pleasure which went on literally night and day; but, most of all, Antioch was famous for the worship of Daphne, whose temple stood five miles out of the town amid laurel groves. The legend was that Daphne was a mortal girl with whom Apollo fell in love. He pursued her, and for her safety Daphne was changed into a laurel bush. The priestesses of the Temple of Daphne were sacred prostitutes, and nightly in the laurel groves the pursuit was re-enacted by the worshippers and the priestesses. 'The morals of Daphne' was a phrase that all the world recognized as indicating loose living. It seems incredible, but nonetheless it is true that it was in a city like this that Christianity took the great stride forward to becoming the religion of the world. We need only think of that to be reminded that no situation is hopeless.

THE WISDOM OF BARNABAS

Acts 11:22-6

> News of this and of what they were doing came to the ears of the church in Jerusalem. So they sent Barnabas out as far as Antioch. When he came and saw the grace of God he was glad, and he exhorted them all to make it the set purpose of their hearts to cleave to the Lord, for he was a good man and full of the Holy Spirit and of faith. He went away to Tarsus to look for Saul, and when he had found him he brought him to Antioch. For a whole year they were guests of the Church there and they instructed a very considerable number of people. And it was at Antioch that the disciples first received the name of Christians.

WHEN the leaders of the church at Jerusalem got word of what was going on at Antioch, they naturally sent someone to investigate the situation.

It was by the grace of God that they sent the man they did. They might have sent someone of a rigid mind who made a god of the law and who was bound by its rules and regulations; but they sent the man with the biggest heart in the Church. Barnabas had already stood by Paul and had vouched for him when everyone was suspicious of him (Acts 9:27). Barnabas had already given proof of his Christian love by his generosity to those who were in need (Acts 4:36–7). When Barnabas saw the Gentiles being swept into the fellowship of the Church, he was glad; but he recognized that someone must be put in charge of this work. That person must be someone with a double background, a Jew brought up in the Jewish tradition but one who could meet the Gentiles on equal terms. That person must be brave – for Antioch was no easy place to be a Christian leader – and must be skilled in argument in order to meet the dual attack of Jews and Gentiles.

Barnabas knew the very person. For nine years or so, we have heard nothing of Paul. The last glimpse we had of him, he was escaping by way of Caesarea to Tarsus (Acts 9:30). No doubt, for these nine years he had been witnessing for Christ in his native town; but now the task for which Paul had been destined was ready for him, and Barnabas with profound wisdom put him in charge of it.

It was in Antioch that the followers of Jesus were first called Christians. The title began as a nickname. The people of Antioch were famous for their facility for finding sarcastic nicknames. Later, the bearded emperor Julian came to visit them, and they nicknamed him 'the Goat'. The word-ending *-iani* means *belonging to the party of*; for instance, *Caesariani* means *belonging to Caesar's party*. Christian means *these Christ-folk*. It was a contemptuous nickname; but the Christians took it and made it known to all the world. By their lives, they made it a name not of contempt but of respect and admiration and even wonder.

HELPING IN TROUBLE

Acts 11:27–30

> In these days, prophets came down from Jerusalem to
> Antioch. One of them called Agabus stood up and,
> through the Holy Spirit, gave a sign that a great famine
> was to come upon the whole land. This happened in the
> reign of Claudius. But each of the disciples, in proportion
> to his resources, fixed upon an amount for a relief fund
> to send to the brethren who lived in Judaea. This they
> did and despatched it to the elders through the hands of
> Barnabas and Saul.

HERE the prophets arrive on the scene. In the early Church,
they were very important. They are mentioned again in
Acts 13:1, 15:32 and 21:9–10. In the early Church, broadly
speaking, there were three sets of leaders. (1) There were the
apostles. Their authority was not confined to one place; their
authority extended through the whole Church; and they were
looked upon as being in a very real sense the successors of
Jesus. (2) There were the *elders*. They were the local officials,
and their authority was confined to the place where they were
set apart. (3) There were the *prophets*.

Their function is to be seen in their name. *Prophet* means
both a *foreteller* and a *forthteller*. They foretold the future;
but, even more, they forthtold the will of God. They had no
settled sphere; they were not attached to any one church. They
were held in the highest honour. The *Teaching of the Twelve
Apostles*, which dates to about AD 100, contains the first service
order book of the Church. The order for the sacrament of the
Lord's Supper is set down, but then it is said that the prophets
are to be allowed to conduct the service as they will. People
knew that the prophets had special gifts. But they were open

to special dangers too. The career of prophet was one which might be undertaken not from the highest but from the lowest of motives. The false prophet existed, the person who simply latched on to the charity of the Church. The same *Teaching of the Twelve Apostles* warns against the prophet who in a vision asks for money or for a meal; it instructs that prophets should always be given hospitality for one night, but says that if they desire to stay longer without working they are false prophets.

This incident is very significant, for it shows that, even at this early stage, people had realized the importance of the unity of the Church. When there was famine in Palestine, the first instinct of the church at Antioch was to help. It was unthinkable that one part of the Church should be in trouble and that another should do nothing about it. They were far away from the congregational outlook; they had that width of vision which saw the Church as a whole.

IMPRISONMENT AND DELIVERANCE

Acts 12:1–11

> About this time, Herod the king began to take hostile action to inflict injury on certain men of the Church. He killed James, John's brother, with the sword. When he saw that this gave pleasure to the Jews, he went to arrest Peter too. (These were the days of unleavened bread.) When he had seized Peter, he put him under arrest. He handed him over to four squads of soldiers to guard, for he wished to bring him before the people after the Passover Feast. So Peter was continuously guarded in prison. Prayer to God for him was earnestly offered by the Church. On the night before Herod was going to bring him before the people, Peter was sleeping between two

soldiers, bound by two chains; and guards kept continuous watch before the door. Now, look you, the Angel of the Lord stood by and a light shone in the house. He struck Peter's side and wakened him and said: 'Rise quickly.' The chains fell from his hands. The angel said to him: 'Gird yourself and put on your sandals.' He did so. He said to him: 'Wrap your cloak round about you and follow me.' So he went out and followed him. And he did not know that what was happening through the angel was real but thought that he was seeing a vision. They went through the first and the second guard and they came to the iron door that led into the city, and it opened to them of its own accord. They went out and proceeded along one street; and thereupon the angel left him. When Peter had recovered his faculties, he said: 'Now I know for sure that the Lord sent his angel and delivered me from the hand of Herod and rescued me from the fate that the people of the Jews looked forward to for me.'

THERE now broke out upon the Church, and especially upon its leaders, a new wave of persecution instigated by King Herod. Let us see briefly the various branches of the family of the Herods in their New Testament connections.

The first of the New Testament Herods is *Herod the Great*, who reigned from about 41 BC to 1 BC. He is the Herod of Matthew 2, who was in power when Jesus was born, who received the wise men from the east and who massacred the children. Herod the Great was married ten times. Those of his family who cross the pages of the New Testament are as follows.

(1) *Herod Philip I*. He was the first husband of the Herodias who was responsible for the death of John the Baptist. He is mentioned, under the name of Philip, in Matthew 14:3, Mark 6:17 and Luke 3:19. He had no official office. He was the father of Salome.

(2) *Herod Antipas*. He was the ruler of Galilee and Peraea. He was the second husband of Herodias and consented to the death of John the Baptist. He was also the Herod to whom Pilate sent Jesus for trial (Luke 23:7ff.).

(3) *Archelaus*. He was the ruler of Judaea, Samaria and Idumaea. He was a thoroughly bad ruler and was deposed and banished. He is mentioned in Matthew 2:22.

(4) *Herod Philip II*. He was the ruler of Ituraea and Trachonitis. He was the founder of Caesarea Philippi, which was named after him. In the New Testament, he is called Philip and is mentioned in Luke 3:1.

(5) Herod the Great had another son called Aristobulus; his mother was Mariamne, a princess who was descended from the great Maccabaean heroes. He was murdered by his own father, but he had a son called *Herod Agrippa*. This is the Herod of our present passage in Acts 12.

(6) To complete the list, we may note that Herod Agrippa was the father of: (a) *Agrippa II*, before whom Paul was examined and before whom he made his famous speech (Acts 25–6); (b) *Bernice*, who appeared with him when Paul was under examination; and (c) *Drusilla*, who was the wife of Felix, the governor before whom Paul was tried (Acts 24:24).

From this family history, it may be seen that Herod Agrippa of this chapter was a direct descendant of the Maccabees through his mother Mariamne. He had been educated at Rome, but he carefully cultivated the good graces of the Jewish people by meticulously keeping the law and all Jewish observances. For these reasons, he was popular with the people; and it was no doubt in order to achieve further popularity with the orthodox Jews that he decided to attack the Christian Church and its leaders. Even his conduct in the arrest of Peter shows his desire to pacify the Jews. The Passover Feast was on 14th

Nisan; for that day and the seven days following, no leaven must be used, and the week was called the days of unleavened bread. During that time, no trial or execution could be carried out, and that is why Herod decided to defer Peter's execution until the week was finished. The great tragedy of this particular wave of persecution was that it was not due to anyone's principles, however misguided; it was due simply to Herod's bid to gain popular favour with the people.

THE JOY OF RESTORATION

Acts 12:12–19

> When Peter had grasped what had happened, he went to the house of Mary, the mother of John, who was surnamed Mark. There a large number had assembled together and were praying. When Peter had knocked at the door of the entrance, a maid servant called Rhoda came to answer the door. She recognized Peter's voice and, in her joy, she did not open the door but ran and told them that Peter stood before the entrance. They said to her: 'You are mad.' She strenuously insisted that it was so; but they kept saying: 'It is his angel.' But Peter waited there knocking. When they opened the door and saw him, they were amazed. With a gesture of his hand he bade them be silent, and he told them the whole story of how the Lord had brought him out of prison. He said: 'Tell these tidings to James and to the brethren.' So he went away to another place. When day came, there was no small disturbance among the soldiers about what had happened to Peter. When Herod had sought for him and did not find him, he examined the guards and ordered them to be led away to execution. And he went down from Judaea to Caesarea and stayed there.

THE greatest precautions had been taken to see that Peter did not escape. He was guarded by four quaternions of soldiers. A quaternion was a squad of four. There were four such squads, because the day and the night were divided into four watches, each of three hours' duration; and each squad was on duty for three hours at a time. Normally a prisoner was chained by the right hand to the guard's left hand; but Peter was chained by both hands to a guard on each side of him, while the two remaining soldiers of the quaternion kept watch at the door. Precautions could go no further. When Peter escaped, the soldiers were led away to execution because it was the law that, if a criminal escaped, the guard should suffer the penalty the prisoner would have suffered.

In this story, we do not necessarily see a miracle. It may well be the story of a thrilling rescue; but, however it happened, the hand of God was most definitely in it.

When Peter escaped, he made his way straight to the house of Mary, the mother of John Mark. From that, we learn that this was the headquarters of the Christian Church. It has indeed been suggested that it was in this very house that the Last Supper was eaten and that it continued to be the meeting place of the disciples in Jerusalem. Note what the Christians were doing. They were praying. When they were up against it, they turned to God.

In this passage, we have the first mention of the man who was the real leader of the Christian church in Jerusalem. Peter instructs them to go and tell the news to James. This is the brother of our Lord. There is a certain mystery about him. In the middle east, it would have been the natural thing for the next brother in age to take on the work of an elder brother who had been killed; but, from the gospels, we learn that Jesus' brothers did not believe in him (John 7:5) and that they actually thought he was mad (Mark 3:21). During his lifetime, James was not a supporter of Jesus. But the risen Christ made a special appearance to James (1 Corinthians 15:7). The apocryphal gospel according to the Hebrews tells that, after the death of Jesus, James made a vow that he would neither eat nor drink until he saw Jesus again, and that Jesus did appear to him. It may well be that what the life of Jesus could not do his death did, and that when James saw his brother die he discovered who he really was and dedicated all his life to serve him. The change in James may well be another great example of the power of the cross to change human lives.

A TERRIBLE END

Acts 12:20–5

> Herod was furious with the people of Tyre and Sidon. But they came to him with a common purpose. They gained the ear of Blastus, the king's chamberlain, and sued for peace because their country was dependent for its sustenance on the king's territory. Upon an agreed day, Herod put on his royal robes and seated himself on a throne and made a speech to them. The people cried out: 'It is the voice of a god and not of a man.' Immediately the Angel of the Lord struck him because he did not give the glory to God. And he was eaten with worms and died.
>
> The word of God increased and was multiplied. And Barnabas and Saul returned from Jerusalem, when they had completed their errand of mercy, and they took with them John who was surnamed Mark.

THERE was at this time a disagreement between Herod and the people of Tyre and Sidon, for whom the quarrel was a serious matter. Their lands lay to the north of Palestine, and in two ways Herod could make things very difficult for them.

If he diverted the trade of Palestine from their ports, their revenues would be seriously impaired. Worse, Tyre and Sidon were dependent for their food supplies on Palestine, and if these supplies were cut off their situation would indeed be serious. So these people succeeded in making their concerns known to Blastus, the king's chamberlain, and in due course a public session was arranged. Josephus, the Jewish historian, describes how, on the second day of the festival, Herod entered the theatre dressed in a robe of silver cloth. The sun glinted on the silver, and the people cried out that this was a god come to them. At once a sudden and terrible illness fell upon Herod from which he never recovered.

Verses 24–5 take us back to Acts 11:27–30. Paul and Barnabas had fulfilled their errand of mercy to the church at Jerusalem and so returned to Antioch, taking with them John Mark.

THE FIRST MISSIONARY JOURNEY

THE thirteenth and fourteenth chapters of Acts tell the story of the first missionary journey. Paul and Barnabas set out from Antioch. Antioch was fifteen miles up the River Orontes, so that they actually sailed from Seleucia, its port. From there they went across the sea to Cyprus, where they preached at Salamis and Paphos. From Paphos they sailed to Perga in Pamphylia. Pamphylia was a low-lying coastal province, and they did not preach there because it did not suit Paul's health. They moved inland and came to Antioch in Pisidia. When things grew too dangerous there, they went ninety miles further on to Iconium. Once again their lives were threatened, and they moved on to Lystra, about twenty miles away. After suffering a very serious and dangerous attack there, they passed on to Derbe, the site of which has not yet been definitely identified. From Derbe they set out home, going back to Lystra, Iconium and Antioch in Pisidia on the way. Having this time preached in Perga in Pamphylia, they boarded a ship from Attalia, the principal port of Pamphylia, and sailed via Seleucia to Antioch. The whole journey occupied about three years.

SENT OUT BY THE HOLY SPIRIT

Acts 13:1–3

> In the local church at Antioch there were prophets and teachers. There were Barnabas, and Simeon who is called Niger, and Lucius from Cyrene, and Manaen, who was brought up with Herod the tetrarch, and Saul. When they were engaged in worshipping God and in fasting, the Holy Spirit said to them: 'Come now, set apart for me Barnabas and Saul for the work to which I have called them in my service.' So after they had fasted and prayed they laid their hands on them and let them go.

THE Christian Church was now poised to take the greatest of all steps. They had decided, quite deliberately, to take the gospel out to all the world. It was a decision taken under the direct guidance of the Holy Spirit. The men and women of the early Church never did what they wanted to do but always did what God wanted them to do.

Prophets and *teachers* had different functions. The prophets were wandering preachers who had given their whole lives to listening for the word of God then taking that word to others. The teachers were those in the local churches whose duty it was to instruct converts in the faith.

It has been pointed out that this list of prophets is symbolic of the universal appeal of the gospel. Barnabas was a Jew from

Cyprus; Lucius came from Cyrene in North Africa; Simeon was also a Jew, but his other name Niger is given and, since this is a Roman name, it shows that he must have moved in Roman circles; Manaen was a man with aristocratic connections; and Paul himself was a Jew from Tarsus in Cilicia and a trained Rabbi. That little group is an example of the unifying influence of Christianity. Individuals from many lands and many backgrounds had discovered the secret of 'togetherness' because they had discovered the secret of Christ.

One extremely interesting speculation has been made. Simeon not improbably came from Africa, for Niger is also an African name. It has been suggested that he is the Simon of Cyrene who carried Jesus' cross (Luke 23:26). It would be a most wonderful thing if the man whose first contact with Jesus was the carrying of the cross – a task which he must have bitterly resented – was one of those directly responsible for sending out the story of the cross to all the world.

SUCCESS IN CYPRUS

Acts 13:4–12

> So when they had been sent out by the Holy Spirit they went down to Seleucia, and from there they sailed away to Cyprus. When they were in Salamis they proclaimed the word of God in the synagogue of the Jews; and they had John as their helper. They went through the whole island as far as Paphos; and there they found a man who was a dealer in magic, a false prophet and a Jew. His name was Bar-Jesus and he was with the proconsul Sergius Paulus, who was an intelligent man. The proconsul summoned Barnabas and Saul and sought to

hear the word of God. Elymas (for such is the translation of his name), the man of magic, opposed them and tried to turn the proconsul away from the faith. But Saul – who is also Paul – filled with the Holy Spirit, fixed his gaze upon him and said: 'You who are full of all deceit and all villainy, you son of the devil, you enemy of righteousness, will you not stop twisting the straight ways of God? And now, look you, the Lord's hand is on you and you will be blind and you will not see the sun for a season.' And thereupon a mist and a darkness fell upon him; and as he groped about he looked for people to lead him by the hand. When the proconsul in astonishment saw what had happened, he believed in the teaching of the Lord.

It was to Cyprus that Paul and Barnabas first went. Barnabas was a native of Cyprus (Acts 4:36), and it would be typical of his gracious heart that he should want to share the treasures of Jesus first of all with his own people. Cyprus was a Roman province, famous for its copper mines and its shipbuilding industry. It was sometimes called Makaria, which means the Happy Isle, because it was held that its climate was so perfect and its resources so varied that it was possible to find everything necessary for a happy life there. Paul never chose an easy way. He and Barnabas preached in Paphos, the capital of the island. Paphos was notorious for its worship of Venus, the goddess of love.

The governor of Cyprus was Sergius Paulus. These were intensely superstitious times – and most great men, even an intelligent man like Sergius Paulus, kept private wizards, fortune-tellers who dealt in magic and spells. Bar-Jesus, or Elymas – an Arabic word which means *the skilful one* – saw that if the governor was won for Christianity he would no longer be needed. Paul dealt effectively with him.

From this point on, Saul is called Paul. In those days, nearly
all Jews had two names. One was a Jewish name, by which
they were known in their own circle; the other was a Greek
name, by which they were known in the wider world.
Sometimes the Greek name translated the Hebrew. So Cephas
is the Hebrew and Peter the Greek for a *rock*; Thomas is the
Hebrew and Didymus the Greek for a *twin*. Sometimes the
name echoed the sound. So Eliakim in Hebrew becomes
Alcimus in Greek, and Joshua becomes Jesus.

So Saul was also Paul. It may well be that from this time
he so fully accepted his mission as the apostle to the Gentiles
that he was determined to use only his Gentile name. If so, it
was the mark that from this time he was launched on the career
for which the Holy Spirit had marked him out and that there
was to be no turning back.

THE DESERTER

Acts 13:13

> Paul and his friends put out to sea from Paphos and came
> to Perga in Pamphylia; and John left them and went back
> to Jerusalem.

WITHOUT his name even being mentioned, this verse pays the
greatest of all tributes to Barnabas. So far, the order has always
been Barnabas and Saul (Acts 13:2). It was Barnabas who
had set out as the leader of this expedition. But now it is Paul
and Barnabas. Paul has assumed the leadership of the expedition; and the lovely thing about Barnabas is that from him
there is no word of complaint. He was a man prepared to take
second place as long as God's work was done.

The main interest of this verse is that it is a strand in the
biography of John Mark – for the John mentioned here is the

man we know better as Mark – who was a deserter who redeemed himself.

Mark was very young. His mother's house seems to have been the centre of the church at Jerusalem (Acts 12:12), and he must always have been close to the centre of the faith. Paul and Barnabas took him with them as their helper, for he was related to Barnabas; but he turned and went home. We will never know why. Perhaps he resented Barnabas being deposed from the leadership; perhaps he was afraid of the proposed journey up into the plateau where Antioch in Pisidia stood, for it was one of the hardest and most dangerous roads in the world; perhaps, because he came from Jerusalem, he had his doubts about this preaching to the Gentiles; perhaps at this stage he was one of those many who are better at beginning things than finishing them; perhaps – as John Chrysostom said in the fourth century – the youth wanted his mother. At any rate, he went.

For a time, Paul found it hard to forgive. When he set out on the second missionary journey, Barnabas wanted to take Mark again; but Paul refused to take the one who had proved a quitter (Acts 15:38), and he and Barnabas parted company for good over it. Then Mark vanishes from history, although tradition says he went to Alexandria and Egypt and founded the church there. When he re-emerges almost twenty years later, he is the man who has redeemed himself. Paul, writing to the Colossians from prison in Rome, tells them to receive Mark if he comes to them. And when he writes to Timothy just before his death, he says: 'Get Mark and bring him with you, for he is useful in my ministry' (2 Timothy 4:11). As the American Baptist, Harry Emerson Fosdick, put it, 'No man need stay the way he is.' By the grace of God, the man who was once a deserter became the writer of a gospel and the man whom, at the end, Paul wanted beside him.

AN ADVENTUROUS JOURNEY
FOR A SICK MAN

Acts 13:14–15

> From Perga they went through the country and arrived
> at Pisidian Antioch. They went into the synagogue on
> the first day of the week and sat down. After the reading
> of the law and the prophets, the rulers of the synagogue
> sent to them with this message: 'Brothers, if you have
> any word of exhortation to say to the people, say on.'

ONE of the amazing things about Acts is the heroism that is
passed over in a sentence. Pisidian Antioch stood on a plateau
3,600 feet above sea level. To get to it, Paul and Barnabas
would have to cross the Taurus range of mountains by one of
the hardest roads in Asia Minor, a road which was also
notorious for robbers and brigands.

But, we are bound to ask, why did they not preach in
Pamphylia? Why did they leave the coast with the word
unproclaimed and set out on that difficult and dangerous way?
Not so very long afterwards, Paul wrote a letter to the people
of Antioch in Pisidia, Iconium, Lystra and Derbe. It is the
letter called the Letter to the Galatians, for all these towns
were in the Roman province of Galatia. In it, he says: 'You
know that it was because of a physical infirmity that I first
announced the gospel to you' (Galatians 4:13). So when he
came to Galatia he was a sick man. Now Paul had what he
described as a thorn in the flesh, which in spite of much prayer
remained with him (2 Corinthians 12:7–8). Many guesses have
been made as to what that thorn was – or *stake* as it probably
should be translated. The oldest tradition is that Paul suffered
from debilitating headaches. And the most likely explanation
is that he was the victim of a virulent recurring malarial fever

which was common on the low coastal strip of Asia Minor. A traveller says that the headache characteristic of this malaria was like a red-hot bar thrust through the forehead; and another likens it to a dentist's drill boring through a person's temple. It is most likely that this malaria attacked Paul in low-lying Pamphylia and that he had to make for the plateau country to shake it off.

Note that it never struck him to turn back. Even when his body was aching, Paul never stopped driving himself forward as an adventurer for Christ.

THE PREACHING OF PAUL

Acts 13:16–41

> Then Paul stood up and made a gesture with his hand and said: 'You Israelites, and you who are God-fearers, listen to this. The God of this people Israel chose out our fathers and he exalted the people when they lived as strangers in the land of Egypt, and with a lofty arm he brought them forth from it. For forty years he bore with their ways in the wilderness. He destroyed seven nations in the land of Canaan and gave them possession of their land, for about 450 years. After that he gave them judges up to the time of Samuel the prophet. Thereafter they asked for a king. And God gave them Saul, the son of Kish, a man of the tribe of Benjamin for forty years. God removed him and raised up David as king for them. In testimony to him, he said: "I found in David, the son of Jesse, a man after my own heart, who will do all things that I wish." It was from the seed of this man, according to his promise, that God brought Jesus, a Saviour for Israel, after John had previously preached, before his coming, a baptism of repentance to all the people of Israel. When John was fulfilling his course, he said:

"What do you suppose me to be? No. I am not he. But, look you, there is coming after me one the shoe of whose feet I am not fit to unloose." Brethren, you who are sons of the race of Abraham, you God-fearers among us, it was for us that the word of this salvation was sent out. Those who live in Jerusalem and their rulers did not recognize this man and they fulfilled the words of the prophets which are read every Sabbath when they condemned him in judgment. Though they found in him no charge which merited the death penalty, they asked Pilate that he should be put to death. When they had completed all that had been written about him, they took him down from the tree and put him in a tomb. But God raised him from the dead and he was seen for many days by those who had come up with him from Galilee to Jerusalem, and they are now witnesses of him to the people; and we bring you the good news of that promise, that was made to the fathers; we tell you that God has fulfilled this to our children by raising up Jesus, even as it stands written in the second psalm: "Thou art My son; this day have I begotten thee." And when he raised him from the dead no longer to return to destruction, he spoke thus: "I will give to you the holy things of David which are faithful" because he says in another passage: "Thou wilt not allow thy holy one to see corruption." For David in his own generation served the will of God and fell asleep, and he was added to his fathers and he *did* see corruption. But the one whom God raised up did not see corruption. Let this be known to you, brethren, that through this man the forgiveness of sins is proclaimed to us. And from all the things from which you could not be acquitted by the law of Moses, everyone who believes in this man is acquitted. So then, take heed lest there come upon you that which was spoken in the prophets – "See, you despisers, and wonder, and be wiped out from

sight, because I work a work in your days, a work in
which you will not believe, even if someone tell it to
you." '

THIS is an extremely important passage because it is the only
full-length report of a sermon by Paul that we possess. When
carefully compared with the sermon of Peter in Acts 2, the
main elements in it are seen to be precisely the same.

(1) Paul insists that the coming of Jesus is the fulfilment
and the end of history. He outlines the national history of the
Jews to show that it reaches its final point in Christ. The Stoics
believed that history simply kept on repeating itself. A modern
cynical verdict is that history is the record of human sins,
mistakes and follies. But the Christian view of history is
optimistic. It is certain that history is always going somewhere
according to the purpose of God.

(2) Paul states the fact that when God's fulfilment came
in Jesus Christ it was not recognized. The poet Robert
Browning said: 'We needs must love the highest when we
see it.' But, by taking our own way and refusing God's way,
we can in the end afflict ourselves with a blindness which
prevents us from seeing. The misuse of free will ends not in
liberty but in ruin.

(3) Although people, in their blind folly, rejected and crucified Jesus, God could not be defeated, and the resurrection is
the proof of the undefeatable purpose and power of God. It is
told that once, on a stormy night when a gale was blowing, a
child said in awe to his father: 'God must have lost grip of his
winds tonight.' The resurrection is the proof that God never
loses grip.

(4) Paul goes on to use a purely Jewish argument. The
resurrection is the fulfilment of prophecy because promises
were made to David which were obviously not fulfilled in
him but which are fulfilled in Christ. Once again, whatever

we make of this argument from prophecy, the fact remains that history is neither circular nor aimless; it looks forward to what must come in God's purpose.

(5) The coming of Christ is good news to one group of people. Hitherto, they had tried to live life according to the law; but no one could ever fulfil that law completely, and therefore anyone who took the matter seriously was always conscious of failure and guilt. But, in Jesus Christ, men and women find that forgiving power which sets them free from the condemnation that should have been theirs and therefore restores real friendship with God.

(6) But what is intended as good news is in fact bad news for another group of people. It simply makes worse the con-demnation of those who have seen it and have disobeyed its summons to belief in Jesus Christ. There is every excuse for someone who has never had a chance, but there is none for the person who has seen the splendour of the offer of God and has rejected it.

TROUBLE AT ANTIOCH

Acts 13:42–52

> As they were going out, they kept asking that these things should be spoken to them on the next Sabbath. When the synagogue service had broken up, many of the Jews and worshipping proselytes followed Paul and Barnabas. They talked with them and tried to persuade them to abide in the grace of God.
>
> On the next Sabbath, nearly the whole city assembled to hear the word of God. When the Jews saw the crowds, they were filled with envy and they argued against what Paul said, making blasphemous statements. Paul and Barnabas, using the boldest language, said: 'It was

> necessary that the word of God should first be spoken
> to you, but since you reject it and since you have proved
> that you are unfit for eternal life, look you, we turn to
> the Gentiles; for thus has the Lord enjoined us: "I have
> appointed you for a light to the Gentiles so that you
> may be for salvation even to the utmost bound of the
> world." ' When the Gentiles heard this, they were glad
> and they glorified the word of God; and all who were
> appointed to eternal life believed. And the word of the
> Lord was carried throughout the whole district. But the
> Jews incited the devout women who were women of
> position, and the chief men of the city, and raised
> persecution against Paul and Barnabas; and they ejected
> them from their bounds. But they shook off the dust of
> their feet against them and went to Iconium. And the
> disciples were filled with joy and the Holy Spirit.

ANTIOCH in Pisidia was a lively and volatile city with a very
mixed population. It had been founded by one of Alexander
the Great's successors about 300 BC. Jews very often flooded
into new cities in order to get in at the start. Since Antioch
was a road centre, it had become a Roman colony in 6 BC. In
the population, there were therefore Greeks, Jews, Romans
and not a few of the native Phrygians, who were an emotional
and unpredictable people. It was the kind of population that
could easily be sparked into actions which could have
devastating effects.

The one thing that infuriated the Jews was that any of God's
privileges could be for the uncircumcised Gentiles. So they
took action. At this time, the Jewish religion had a special
attraction for women. In nothing was the ancient world more
lax than in sexual morality. Family life was rapidly breaking
down, and the worst sufferers were women. The Jewish
religion preached a purity of ethic and cleanness of life. Round

the synagogues gathered many women, often of high social position, who found in this teaching just what they longed for. Many of these women became converts to Judaism; still more were God-fearers. The Jews persuaded them to encourage their husbands, who were often men in influential positions, to take steps against the Christian preachers. The inevitable result was persecution. Antioch became unsafe for Paul and Barnabas, and they had to go.

The Jews were intent on keeping their privileges to themselves. From the beginning, the Christians saw their privileges as something to be shared. As has been said, 'The Jews saw the Gentiles as straw to be burned; Jesus saw them as a harvest to be reaped for God.' And similarly his Church must have a vision of a world for Christ.

ON TO ICONIUM

Acts 14:1–7

It happened in Iconium that they went in the same way into the synagogue of the Jews and spoke to such effect that a great crowd of the Jews and of the Greeks believed. But the Jews who did not believe inflamed the minds of the Gentiles against the brethren. So then, they spent some considerable time boldly speaking in the name of the Lord, who bore witness to the word of his grace by causing signs and wonders to happen through their hands. The population of the city was torn in two. Some sided with the Jews and some with the apostles. When the Gentiles and the Jews with their leaders combined in a movement to assault and stone them, they discovered what was afoot and fled for safety to the cities of Lycaonia, Lystra and Derbe, and the surrounding district. And there they continued to preach the good news.

PAUL and Barnabas went on to Iconium, about ninety miles from Antioch. It was a city so ancient that it claimed to be older than Damascus. In the distant past, it had had a king called Nannacus, and the phrase 'since the days of Nannacus' was a well-known phrase meaning 'from the beginning of time'. As usual, they began in the synagogue, and as usual they had some success; but the jealous Jews stirred up the crowd, and once again Paul and Barnabas had to move on.

It has to be noted that Paul and Barnabas were more and more taking their lives in their hands. What was proposed in Iconium was nothing other than a lynching. The further Paul and Barnabas went, the further they moved from civilization. In the more civilized cities, their lives at least were safe because Rome kept order; but, out in the wilds, Paul and Barnabas were constantly under the threat of mob violence from the excitable Phrygian crowds stirred up by the Jews. These two were brave men; and it always takes courage to be a Christian.

MISTAKEN FOR GODS AT LYSTRA

Acts 14:8–18

> There was a man who sat in Lystra who had no power in his feet. He had been a cripple from his birth, and he had never walked. He was in the habit of listening to Paul speaking. Paul fixed his gaze on him. He saw that he had faith that he could be cured, and he said to him in a loud voice: 'Stand up straight on your feet.' He leaped up and kept walking about. When the crowds saw what Paul had done, they exclaimed in the Lycaonian dialect: 'The gods have taken the form of men and have come down to us.' They called Barnabas, Zeus; and Paul, Hermes, because he was the leader in speaking. The priest of Zeus whose shrine is in front of

the city brought oxen and wreaths to the gates, and he and the crowd wished to offer sacrifice to them. But when the apostles Barnabas and Paul heard this, they rent their clothes and rushed in among the people shouting: 'Men, what is this you are doing? We too are men of like passions with you. We are bringing you the good news which tells you to turn from these empty things to the living God, who made heaven and earth and sea and all that is in them. In past generations he allowed all nations to go their own way. And yet he never left himself without a witness, for he was kind to men, and he gave you rain from heaven and the fruitful seasons and he filled your hearts with food and gladness.' As they said these things, they could hardly stop the crowds sacrificing to them.

At Lystra, Paul and Barnabas were involved in a strange incident. The explanation of their being taken for gods lies in the legendary history of Lycaonia. The people round Lystra told a story that once Zeus and Hermes had come to this earth in disguise. No one in all the land would give them hospitality until at last two old peasants, Philemon and his wife Baucis, took them in. As a result, the whole population except for Philemon and Baucis was wiped out by the gods, and Philemon and Baucis were made the guardians of a splendid temple and were turned into two great trees when they died. So, when Paul healed the crippled man, the people of Lystra were determined not to make the same mistake again. Barnabas must have had a noble presence, so they took him for Zeus, the king of the gods. Hermes was the messenger of the gods; and, since Paul was the speaker, they called him Hermes.

This passage is especially interesting because it gives us Paul's approach to those who were without any Jewish background to which he could appeal because they were followers of Greek and Roman gods. With such people, he started from nature to get to the God who was behind it all. He started from the here and now to get to the there and then. We do well to remember that the world is the garment of the living God. It is told that once, as they sailed in the Mediterranean, Napoleon's party were discussing God. In the talk, they eliminated God altogether. Napoleon had been silent, but now he lifted his hand and pointed to the sea and the sky. 'Gentlemen,' he said, 'who made all this?'

THE COURAGE OF PAUL

Acts 14:19–20

> There came certain Jews from Antioch and Iconium. They won over the crowds, and they stoned Paul and dragged him outside the city, for they thought he was dead. While the disciples stood in a circle round him, he got up and he went into the city; and on the next day with Barnabas he went away to Derbe.

In the midst of all the excitement at Lystra, some Jews arrived. They may have been there for one of two reasons. They may have been deliberately following Paul and Barnabas in a determined attempt to undo the work that they were doing. Or they may have been corn merchants. The region round Lystra was a great corn-growing area, and they may have come to buy corn for the cities of Iconium and Antioch. If so, they would be shocked and angry to find Paul still preaching and would very naturally stir up the people against him.

Lystra was a Roman colony, but it was an outpost. Nevertheless, when the people saw what they had done, they were afraid. That is why they dragged what they thought was Paul's dead body out of the city. They were afraid of the strong hand of Roman justice, and they were trying to get rid of Paul's body in order to escape the consequences of their riot.

The outstanding feature of this story is the sheer courage of Paul. When he came to his senses, his first act was to go straight back into the city where he had been stoned. It was the great Methodist John Wesley's advice: 'Always look a mob in the face.' There could be no braver thing than Paul's going back immediately among those who had tried to murder him. An action like that would have more effect than 100 sermons. People were bound to ask themselves where Paul got the courage to act in such a way.

CONFIRMING THE CHURCH

Acts 14:21-8

> When they had preached the good news to that city and had made a considerable number of disciples, they returned to Lystra and to Iconium and to Antioch. As they went, they strengthened the souls of the disciples and urged them to abide in the faith, saying: 'It is through many an affliction that we must enter into the kingdom of God.' In each church they chose elders, and, when they had prayed with fasting, they offered them to the Lord in whom they had believed. When they had gone through Pisidia, they came to Pamphylia. When they had spoken the word in Perga, they went down to Attaleia. From there they sailed away to Antioch, from which they had been handed over to the grace of God for the work which they had completed. On their arrival there, when they had called a meeting of the church, they told them the story of all that God had done with them and that he had opened the door of faith to the Gentiles. They spent a long time with the disciples.

IN this passage, there are three notable insights into the mind of Paul.

(1) There is his utter honesty to the people who had chosen to become Christians. He told them frankly that it was through many afflictions that they would have to enter into the kingdom of God. He offered them no easy way. He acted on the principle that Jesus had come 'not to make life easy but to make people great'.

(2) On the return journey, Paul set apart elders in all the little groups of newly made Christians. He showed that it was his conviction that Christianity must be lived in a fellowship. As one of the great Christian fathers put it, 'No man can have God for his father unless he has the Church for his mother.' As John Wesley put it, 'No man ever went to heaven alone; he must either find friends or make them.' From the very beginning, it was Paul's aim not only to make individual Christians but also to build these individuals into a Christian fellowship.

(3) Paul and Barnabas never thought that it was their strength which had achieved anything. They spoke of what God had done with them. They regarded themselves only as fellow labourers with God. After the great victory of Agincourt, the English king, Henry V, forbade any songs to be composed and ordered that all the glory should be given to God. We begin to have the right idea of Christian service when we work not for our own honour but from the conviction that we are tools in the hand of God.

THE CRUCIAL PROBLEM

THE continual stream of Gentiles into the Church produced a problem which had to be solved. The sense of identity for all Jews was founded on the fact that they saw themselves as the chosen people. In effect, they believed not only that the Jews were the special possession of God but also that God was the special possession of the Jews. The problem was this. Before Gentiles became members of the Christian Church, was it necessary for them to be circumcised and to take upon themselves the law of Moses? In other words – must the Gentiles, before they became Christians, first become Jews? Or, could Gentiles be received into the Church in their own right?

Even if that question could be settled, there arose another problem. The strict Jews could have no dealings with Gentiles. They could not have Gentiles as guests nor be their guests. They would not, as far as possible, even do business with them. So, even if Gentiles were allowed into the Church, how far could Jews and Gentiles associate in the ordinary social life of the Church?

These were the problems which had to be solved. The solution was not easy. But, in the end, the Church took the decision that there should be no difference between Jews and Gentiles at all. The fifteenth chapter of Acts tells of the Council of Jerusalem whose decisions were the charter of freedom for the Gentiles.

A PROBLEM BECOMES ACUTE

Acts 15:1-5

> Some men came down from Judaea and tried to teach the brethren: 'If you are not circumcised according to the practice of Moses, you cannot be saved.' When Paul and Barnabas had a great dispute and argument with them, they arranged for Paul and Barnabas and some others to go up to Jerusalem to the apostles and elders to get this question settled. So they were sent on their way by the Church, and they passed through Phoenicia

and Samaria telling the story of the conversion of the Gentiles; and they brought great joy to all the brethren. When they arrived at Jerusalem, they were received by the Church and the apostles and the elders, and they told the story of all that God had done with them. But some men of the school of the Pharisees, who were converts, rose and said: 'It is necessary to circumcise them and to enjoin them to keep the law of Moses.'

I⊤ was almost by accident that the most epoch-making things were happening in Antioch so that the gospel was being preached both to Jews and to Gentiles and they were living together in fellowship. There were certain Jews to whom all this was quite unthinkable. They could never forget the position of the Jews as the chosen people. They were quite willing for the Gentiles to come into the Church, but on the condition that first they became Jews. If this attitude had prevailed, Christianity would have become nothing other than a sect of Judaism. Some of these more narrow-minded Jews came down to Antioch and tried to persuade the converts that they would lose everything unless they first accepted Judaism. Paul and Barnabas argued strongly against this, and matters were at a deadlock.

There was only one way out. An appeal must be made to Jerusalem, the headquarters of the Church, for a ruling. The case which Paul and Barnabas put forward was simply the story of what had happened. They were prepared to let the facts speak for themselves. But some of the Pharisees who had become Christians insisted that all converts must be circumcised and keep the law.

The principle at stake was quite simple and completely fundamental. Was the gift of God for the select few or for all the world? If we possess it ourselves, are we to look on it as a privilege or as a responsibility? The problem may not meet us nowadays in precisely the same way; but there still exist divisions between class and class, between nation and nation, between colour and colour. We fully realize the true meaning of Christianity only when all middle walls of partition are broken down.

PETER STATES THE CASE

Acts 15:6–12

> The apostles and elders met together to investigate this question. After a great deal of discussion, Peter stood up and said: 'Brethren, you know that in the early days God made his choice among us, so that through my mouth the Gentiles should hear the good news and believe. And God, who knows men's hearts, bore his own witness to them by giving them the Holy Spirit just as he had done to us too. He made no distinction between us and them, for he purified their hearts by faith. So why do you now tempt God by placing on the necks of the disciples a yoke which neither our fathers nor we had the strength to bear? But it is through the grace of Jesus Christ that we believe that we have been saved in exactly the same way as they too have been.' The whole assembly was silent and listened to Barnabas and Paul as they told the story of all the signs and wonders God had done among the heathen through them.

In answer to the stricter Jews, Peter reminded them how he himself had been responsible for the reception of Cornelius into the Church ten years before this. The proof that he had acted rightly was that God had granted his Holy Spirit to these very Gentiles who had been received. As far as the law's claims went, they might have been ceremonially unclean; but by his Spirit God had cleansed their hearts. The attempt to obey the law's many different kinds of command and so to earn salvation was a losing battle in which everyone was inadequate. There was only one way – the acceptance of the free gift of the grace of God in an act of self-surrendering faith.

Peter went right to the heart of the question. In this whole dispute, the deepest of principles was involved. Can we *earn* the favour of God? Or must we admit our own helplessness and be ready in humble faith to accept what the grace of God gives? In effect, the Jewish party said: 'Religion means earning God's favour by keeping the law.' Peter said: 'Religion consists in casting ourselves on the grace of God.' Underlying the debate is the difference between a religion of works and a religion of grace. Peace will never come until we realize that we can never put God in our debt, and that all we can do is take what God in his grace gives. The paradox of Christianity is that the way to victory is through surrender; and the way to power is through admitting one's own helplessness.

THE LEADERSHIP OF JAMES

Acts 15:13–21

> After they had been silent, James replied: 'Brothers, listen to me. Simeon has told you how God first made provision for the Gentiles, to take from them a people for his name. With this the words of the prophets agree, as it stands written: "After these things I will return and I will build again the tabernacle of David which has fallen. I will build its ruins again, and again I will set it upright, so that the rest of mankind will seek the Lord, even all the Gentiles who are called by my name" – this is what the Lord says, making these things known from the beginning of the world. Therefore for my part, it is

my judgment that we stop making things difficult for
the Gentiles who turn to God, but that we send them a
letter to keep themselves from the contaminations
offered to idols, from fornication, from things strangled
and from blood. For Moses from of old has those who
proclaim his teaching in every city, for his works are
read in the synagogues every Sabbath.'

WE may well believe that the matter of the reception of the
Gentiles hung in the balance; then James spoke. He was the
leader of the Jerusalem church. His leadership was not a
formal office; it was a moral leadership conceded to him
because he was an outstanding individual. He was the brother
of Jesus. He had had a special resurrection appearance all to
himself (1 Corinthians 15:7). He was a pillar of the Church
(Galatians 1:19). His knees were said to be as hard as a
camel's because he knelt in prayer so often and so long. He
was so good a man that he was called James the Just. Further
– and this was all-important – he himself was a rigorous
observer of the law. If such a man should come down on the
side of the Gentiles, then all was well; and he did, declaring
that the Gentiles should be allowed into the Church without
anything further standing in their way.

Even then, the matter of ordinary social interaction came
in. How could a strict Jew have dealings with a Gentile? To
make things easier, James suggested certain regulations that
Gentiles ought to keep.

They must abstain from the contamination of idols. One of
the great problems of the early Church was that of meat offered
to idols. Paul deals with it at length in 1 Corinthians 8–9.
When a sacrifice was offered at a temple to one of the Greek
or Roman gods, often only a small part of the meat was sacrificed. Most of the rest was returned to the worshipper to make
a feast with friends, often in the Temple precincts, sometimes

at home. The priests received the remainder, which was then sold for ordinary purposes. No Christian could risk pollution by eating such meat, because it had been offered to an idol.

They must abstain from fornication. It has been said that chastity was the only completely new virtue that Christianity brought into the world. In an impure world, Christians had to be pure.

They must abstain from things strangled and from blood. To Jews, the blood was the life and the life belonged to God alone, because when the blood flowed away life ebbed away too. Therefore all Jewish meat was killed and treated in such a way that the blood was drained off. The Gentile practice of not draining the blood from a slaughtered animal was obnoxious to strict Jews, as was the method of killing by strangulation. So the Gentiles are ordered to eat only meat prepared in the Jewish way.

Had these simple regulations not been observed, there could have been no dealings between Jews and Gentiles; but their observance destroyed the last barrier. Within the Church, the principle was established that Jews and Gentiles were one.

THE DECREE GOES OUT

Acts 15:22–35

> Then the apostles and the elders together with the whole Church took a decision to choose men from their number and to send them to Antioch with Paul and Barnabas. They chose Judas who is called Barsabas and Silas, men who were leaders among the brethren, and they sent a written message by their hand. 'The apostles and the elders, brethren, to the brethren from the Gentiles who are throughout Antioch and Syria and Cilicia – greetings. We have heard that some who came from us have

disturbed you with their words in an attempt to upset
your souls. They were not acting under our instructions.
We have therefore decided, when we were met together,
to choose men and to send them to you, with our beloved
Barnabas and Paul, who are men who have devoted their
lives for the name of the Lord Jesus Christ. We have
therefore despatched Judas and Silas to you to tell you
the same things by word of mouth. It was the decision
of the Holy Spirit and of us to place no further burden
on you other than the rules which are necessary – that
you should keep yourselves from things offered to idols,
from blood, from things strangled and from fornication.
If you keep yourselves from these things, you will be
doing well. Farewell.' So these were sent away and came
down to Antioch. They called the congregation together
and delivered the letter to them. When they had read it
they rejoiced at the message of comfort. Judas and Silas,
who were themselves prophets, exhorted the brethren
with many an address and strengthened them. After
spending some time there, they were sent away with
every good wish for their welfare from the brethren to
those who had sent them. But Paul and Barnabas with
certain others, too, stayed in Antioch teaching and telling
the good news of the word of the Lord.

ONCE the Church had come to its decision, it acted with both
efficiency and courtesy. The terms of the decision were
embodied in a letter. But the letter was sent by no ordinary
messenger; it was entrusted to Judas and to Silas, who went
to Antioch with Paul and Barnabas. If Paul and Barnabas had
come back alone, their enemies might have doubted that they
brought back a correct message; Judas and Silas were official
messengers and guarantors of the reality of the decision. The
Church was wise in sending a person as well as a letter. One
of the earliest Christian writers declared that he had learned

more from the living and abiding voice than from any amount of reading. A letter could have sounded coldly official; but the words of Judas and Silas added a friendly warmth that the bare reception of a letter could never have achieved. Any amount of trouble might be avoided on many occasions if only a personal visit were paid instead of someone being content with sending a letter.

PAUL TAKES TO THE ROAD AGAIN

Acts 15:36–41

> Some time after, Paul said to Barnabas: 'Come now, let us go back and visit the brethren in every city in which we preached the word of the Lord, so that we may see how things are going with them.' Barnabas wished to take John who was called Mark along with them; but Paul did not think it right to take with them one who had deserted them in Pamphylia and had not gone with them to the work. There was so sharp a difference of opinion that they were separated from each other and Barnabas took Mark with him and sailed away to Cyprus; but Paul chose Silas and went off when he had been commended by the brethren to the grace of the Lord. He went through Syria and Cilicia strengthening the churches.

PAUL was a born adventurer and could never stay long in the one place. He decided to take to the road again; but the preparations for the journey ended in a tragic rift. Barnabas wanted to take John Mark, but Paul would have nothing to do with the man who had deserted him in Pamphylia. The difference between them was so sharp that they split up, never to work with each other again. It is impossible to say whether

Barnabas or Paul was right. But this much is certain: Mark was supremely fortunate that he had a friend like Barnabas. In the end, as we know, Mark became the man who redeemed himself. It may well have been the friendship of Barnabas which gave Mark back his self-respect and made him determined to make good. It is a great thing to have someone who believes in us. Barnabas believed in Mark, and in the end Mark justified that belief.

THE SECOND MISSIONARY JOURNEY

THE narrative of Paul's second missionary journey, which occupied him for about three years, is given in the section of Acts which extends from 15:36 to 18:23. It began from Antioch. Paul first made a tour of the churches of Syria and Cilicia. Then he revisited the churches in the regions of Derbe, Lystra, Iconium and Pisidian Antioch. There followed a period when he could not see the way ahead clearly. That time of uncertainty ended with the vision at Troas. From Troas, Paul crossed to Neapolis and from there went on to Philippi. From Philippi, he moved on to Thessalonica and Beroea. From there, he went to Athens and then on to Corinth, where he spent about eighteen months. From Corinth, he travelled to Jerusalem by way of Ephesus and finally back to Antioch, his starting point. The great step forward is that, with this journey, Paul's activity passed beyond Asia Minor and entered Europe.

A SON IN THE FAITH

Acts 16:1-5

> Paul arrived at Derbe and Lystra and, look you, there
> was a disciple there called Timothy. He was the son
> of a Jewish woman who was a believer, but his father

was Greek. The brethren in Lystra and Iconium were witnesses to his worth. Paul wished him to go out with him, and he took him and circumcised him because of the Jews who were in these places, for they all knew that his father was Greek. As they made their way through the cities, they handed over to them the decisions which had been arrived at by the apostles and elders in Jerusalem, that they should observe them. The churches were strengthened in the faith and increased in number every day.

It was five years since Paul had preached in Derbe and Lystra; but, when he returned, his heart must have been gladdened, for a young man who was to be very dear to him had emerged. It was only natural that Paul should be looking for someone to take Mark's place. He was always well aware of the necessity of training a new generation for the work that lay ahead. In Timothy, he found just the kind of person he wanted. On the face of it, it is something of a problem that Paul circumcised Timothy, for he had just won a battle in which circumcision had been declared unnecessary. The reason was that Timothy was a Jew, and Paul had never said that circumcision was not necessary for Jews. It was the Gentiles who were freed from the ceremonies of the Jewish way of life.

In fact, by accepting Timothy as a Jew, Paul showed just how liberated from Jewish thought he was. Timothy was the son of a mixed marriage. The strict Jews would refuse to accept that as a marriage at all; in fact, if a Jewish girl married a Gentile boy or a Jewish boy married a Gentile girl, they would regard that Jewish boy or girl as dead – so much so, that sometimes a funeral was actually carried out. By accepting the child of such a marriage as a fellow Jew, Paul showed how definitely he had broken down all national barriers.

Timothy was a young man with a great heritage. He had had a good mother and a good grandmother (2 Timothy 1:5). Often in the days to come, he was to be Paul's messenger (1 Corinthians 4:17; 1 Thessalonians 3:2–6). He was at Rome with Paul when the apostle was in prison (Philippians 1:1, 2:19; Colossians 1:1; Philemon 1). Timothy had a very special relationship with Paul. When Paul wrote to the Corinthians (1 Corinthians 4:17), he called him his beloved son. When he wrote to the Philippians, he said that there was no one whose mind was so much at one with his own (Philippians 2:19–20). It seems very likely that Paul saw in Timothy the successor who would take his place when he had to lay down his work. Happy indeed are those to whom it is given to see the result of their training in others who can take up the burden when they lay it down.

THE GOSPEL COMES TO EUROPE

Acts 16:6–10

> They went through the Phrygian and Galatian territory, but they were prevented by the Holy Spirit from speaking the word in Asia. When they had gone through Mysia they tried to go into Bithynia; and the Spirit of Jesus did not allow them to do so. So they passed by Mysia and came down to Troas. During the night, a vision appeared to Paul. A man from Macedonia stood and urged him: 'Cross over into Macedonia and help us.' When he saw the vision, he immediately sought to go forth into Macedonia, for we reckoned that God had called us to tell the good news to them.

FOR a time, all doors seemed shut to Paul. It must have seemed strange to him that he was barred from the Roman province of Asia by the Holy Spirit; it contained Ephesus and all the recipients of the letters to the seven churches in the book of Revelation. Bithynia, too, was closed to him. How did the Holy Spirit send his message to Paul? It may have been by the word of a prophet; it may have been by a vision; it may have been by some inner and inescapable conviction. But there is the possibility that what kept Paul from journeying into these provinces was ill health, the consequence of that thorn in his flesh.

What makes that quite likely is that in verse 10, suddenly and without warning, there emerges a 'we' passage. The story begins to be told not in the third person but in the first person. That tells us that Luke was there, an eyewitness and a companion of Paul. Why should he so suddenly emerge on the scene? Luke was a doctor. What is more likely than that he met Paul then because Paul, who had fallen ill and so was barred from making the journeys he would like to make, needed his professional services? If this is so, it is instructive to reflect that Paul took even his weakness and his pain as a messenger from God.

It was the sight of a man from Macedonia which finally gave Paul his guidance. Who was this man Paul saw in the vision? Some think it was Luke himself, for Luke may have been a Macedonian. Some think the question should not be asked, since dreams need no explanations like that. But there is a most attractive theory. There was one man who had succeeded in conquering the world. That was Alexander the Great. Now it would seem that the whole situation was designed to make Paul remember Alexander. The full name of Troas was Alexandrian Troas, after Alexander. Just across the sea was Philippi, named after Alexander's father. Further on was Thessalonica, named after Alexander's half-sister. The district was filled with memories of Alexander; and Alexander was the man who had said that his aim was 'to marry the east to the west' and so make one world. It may well be that there came to Paul the vision of Alexander, the man who had conquered the world, and that this vision gave Paul a new impulse towards making one world for Christ.

EUROPE'S FIRST CONVERT

Acts 16:11–15

> When we had set sail from Troas, we had a straight run to Samothrace. On the next day we reached Neapolis, and from there we came to Philippi, which is the chief city of that section of Macedonia and a Roman colony. We spent some days in this city. On the Sabbath day, we went outside the gates along the riverside where we believed there was a place of prayer. We sat down and were talking with the women who met together there. A woman whose name was Lydia, who was a purple-seller from the city of Thyatira, who reverenced God, listened to us. God opened her heart so that she gave heed to the things said by Paul. When she and her household had been baptized, she urged us: 'If you judge me to be faithful to the Lord, come into my house and stay there.' And she pressed us to do so.

NEAPOLIS – the modern Kavalla – was the seaport of Philippi. Philippi had a long history. Once it had been called Crenides, which means 'the Springs'. But Philip of Macedon, the father of Alexander, had fortified it as a barrier against the Thracians and had given it his own name. At one time it had possessed famous gold mines, but by Paul's time these had been exhausted. Later it had been the scene of one of the most famous battles in the world, when Augustus won for himself the Roman Empire.

Philippi was a Roman colony. Roman colonies were usually strategic centres. In them, Rome planted little groups of army veterans who had completed their military service. They wore the Roman form of dress, spoke the Roman language and used the Roman laws, no matter where they were. Nowhere was there greater pride in Roman citizenship than in these outposts of Rome.

In Philippi, there was no synagogue from which to start. But, where the Jews were unable to have a synagogue, they had a place of prayer – and these places of prayer were usually by the riverside. On the Sabbath, Paul and his friends made their way there and talked with the women who met in that place.

The extraordinary thing about Paul's work in Philippi is the amazing cross-section of the population that was won for Christ. Lydia came from the very top end of the social scale; she was a purple-merchant. The purple dye had to be gathered drop by drop from a certain shellfish and so was extremely costly. Lydia, wealthy woman that she was, was won for Christ.

Her immediate reaction was to offer the hospitality of her house to Paul and his friends. When Paul is describing the Christian character, he says that the Christian should 'extend hospitality' (Romans 12:13). When Peter is urging Christian duty upon his converts, he tells them: 'Be hospitable to one another without complaining' (1 Peter 4:9). A Christian home is one where the door is always open.

THE DEMENTED SLAVE GIRL

Acts 16:16–24

> When we were on our way to the place of prayer, it happened that a certain slave girl who had a spirit which

made her able to give oracles met us. By her soothsaying she provided much gain for her owners. As she followed Paul and us, she kept shouting: 'These men are the slaves of the most high God and they are proclaiming the way of salvation to you.' She kept doing this for many days. Paul was vexed at this, and he turned and said to the spirit: 'In the name of Jesus Christ, I order you to come out of her.' And it came out that very hour.

When her owners saw that their hope of gain was gone, they laid hands on Paul and Silas and dragged them to the city square to the magistrates. So they brought them to the chief magistrates and said: 'These men, who are Jews, are disturbing the whole city and are proclaiming customs which it is not right for us who are Romans to receive.' The crowd came together against them. The chief magistrates tore off their clothes and ordered them to be scourged with rods. When they had laid many blows upon them, they threw them into prison with instructions to the jailer to guard them securely. When he received such an order, he flung them into the inner prison and secured their feet in the stocks.

IF Lydia came from the top end of the social scale, this slave girl came from the bottom. She was what was called a Pytho, that is, a person who could give oracles to guide people about the future. She was insane – and the ancient world had a strange respect for such people because, they said, the gods had taken away their wits in order to put the mind of the gods into them. She was probably also gifted with a natural aptitude for ventriloquism. She had fallen into the hands of unscrupulous men who used her misfortune for their gain. When Paul cured her of her madness, these men felt not joy at her restoration to health but fury that their source of revenue was gone. They were astute men. They played on the natural anti-semitism of the crowd; and they appealed to the pride in things Roman which was characteristic of a Roman colony, and they succeeded in having Paul and Silas arrested. Not only were they arrested; they were put in the inner prison in the stocks. It may be that not only their feet but also their hands and their necks were held in the stocks.

The tragic thing is that Paul and Silas were arrested and ill-treated for doing good. Whenever Christianity attacks vested interests, trouble follows. It is a human characteristic that if people's pockets are affected they are up in arms. It is everyone's duty to ask: 'Is the money I am earning worth the price? Do I earn it by serving or by exploiting my neighbours?' Often, the greatest obstacle to the crusade of Christ is human selfishness.

THE PHILIPPIAN JAILER

Acts 16:25–40

> About midnight, Paul and Silas were praying and singing hymns to God, and the prisoners were listening to them. Suddenly there was a great earthquake so that the foundations of the prison were shaken. Immediately the doors were opened and everyone's bonds were loosed. When the jailer woke up and saw the doors of the prison standing open, he drew his sword and he was going to kill himself, for he thought that the prisoners had escaped. But Paul shouted to him: 'Do yourself no harm, for we are all here.' He called for a light and rushed in. He fell in terror before Paul and Silas and brought them out and said: 'Sirs, what must I do to be saved?' They said: 'Believe on the Lord Jesus and you and your house will be saved.' And they spoke the Lord's word to him together with all in his house. And that very hour he took them and washed their weals and he and his

household were immediately baptized. He brought them into his house and set a meal before them and he rejoiced with all his house when he had believed in God.

When day came, the chief magistrates sent their officers saying: 'Let these men go.' The jailer brought the message to Paul: 'The chief magistrates have sent word that you are to be released. So now, go out and go your way in peace.' But Paul said to them: 'They beat us and they put us into prison although we never had a trial – and we are Romans. And now are they going to put us out secretly? Certainly not! Let them come themselves and bring us out.' The officers told the chief magistrates what Paul had said. They were afraid when they heard that they were Romans. So they came and requested them and brought them out and asked them to leave the city. When they had come out of prison, they visited Lydia. They saw the brethren and exhorted them and went away.

IF Lydia came from the top end of the social scale and the slave girl from the bottom, the Roman jailer was one of the sturdy middle class who made up the Roman civil service; and so in these three the whole range within society was complete.

Let us look first at the *scene* of this passage. This was a district where earthquakes were by no means uncommon. The door was locked by a wooden bar falling into two slots, and the stocks were similarly fastened. The earthquake shook the bar free, and the prisoners were freed from their chains and the door was open. The jailer was about to kill himself because Roman law said that if a prisoner escaped the jailer must suffer the penalty the prisoner would have suffered.

Let us look at the *characters*.

First, there is Paul. We note three things about Paul. (1) He could sing hymns when he was confined in the stocks in the inner prison at midnight. The one thing you can never take away from a Christian is God and the presence of Jesus Christ. With God there is freedom even in a prison, and even at midnight there is light. (2) He was quite willing to open the door of salvation to the jailer who had shut the door of the prison on him. There was never a grudge in Paul's nature. He could preach to the person who had chained him into the stocks. (3) He could stand on his dignity. He claimed his rights as a Roman citizen. To scourge a Roman citizen was a crime punishable by death. But Paul was not standing on his dignity for his own sake but for the sake of the Christians he was leaving behind in Philippi. He wanted it to be seen that they were not without influential friends.

Second, there is the jailer. The interesting thing about the jailer is that he immediately proved his conversion by his deeds. No sooner had he turned to Christ than he washed the wounds upon the prisoners' backs and gave them food. Unless our Christianity makes us kind, it is not real. Unless our declared change of heart is guaranteed by our change of deeds, it is superficial and false.

IN THESSALONICA

Acts 17:1–9

> When they had taken the road through Amphipolis and Apollonia, they came to Thessalonica, where there was a synagogue of the Jews. Paul, as his custom was, went in to them and, for three Sabbaths, he debated with them from the Scriptures, opening the Scriptures to them and presenting the evidence that Christ had to suffer and to rise from the dead – 'and this man', he said, 'is the Christ, Jesus whom I proclaim to you'. Some of them believed and threw in their lot with Paul and Silas. Thus it was

with many of the worshipping Greeks and with a considerable number of women who belonged to the most influential ranks of society. The Jews resented this. They got hold of some of the low characters who haunted the market place and they formed a mob and set the city in an uproar. They surged up to Jason's house and kept demanding that they should bring them before the people. When they did not find them, they dragged Jason and some of the brethren to the city magistrates, shouting: 'These men who have upset the civilized world have arrived here too; and Jason has received them as his guests. These are all teaching against the decrees of Caesar, for they say that there is another emperor – Jesus.' They disturbed the mob and the chief magistrates as they heard this. So they took surety from Jason and the others and let them go.

THE coming of Christianity to Thessalonica was an event of prime importance. The great Roman road from the Adriatic sea to the middle east was called the Egnatian Way; and the main street of Thessalonica was actually part of that road. If Christianity was firmly founded in Thessalonica, it could spread both east and west along that road until it became a highway of the progress of the kingdom of God.

The first verse of this chapter is an extraordinary example of economy of writing. It sounds like a pleasant stroll; but in point of fact Philippi was thirty-three miles from Amphipolis; Amphipolis was thirty miles from Apollonia; and Apollonia was thirty-seven miles from Thessalonica. A journey of over 100 miles is dismissed in a sentence.

As usual, Paul began his work in the synagogue. His great success was not so much among the Jews as among the Gentiles attached to the synagogue. This infuriated the Jews, for they looked on these Gentiles as part of their community, and here was Paul stealing them before their very eyes. The

Jews stooped to the lowest methods to hinder Paul. First, they stirred up the rabble. Then, when they had dragged Jason and his friends before the magistrates, they charged the Christian missionaries with preaching political rebellion. They knew their charge to be a lie, and yet it is expressed in terms that were full of significance. 'Those', they said, 'who are upsetting the civilized world have arrived here' (Authorized Version: 'these men who have turned the world upside down'). The Jews had not the slightest doubt that Christianity was supremely *effective*. The New Testament scholar, T. R. Glover, quoted with delight the saying of the child who remarked that the New Testament ended with *Revolutions*. When Christianity really goes into action, it inevitably causes a revolution both in the life of the individual and in the life of society.

ON TO BEROEA

Acts 17:10–15

> The brethren immediately sent Paul and Silas away to Beroea by night. When they arrived there, they came into the synagogue of the Jews. These were men of finer character than those in Thessalonica, and they received the word with all eagerness. They daily examined the Scriptures to see if these things were so. Many of them believed, as did a considerable number of well-to-do Greek women and men. When the Jews of Thessalonica knew that the word of God was preached by Paul in Beroea, they came there too in an attempt to stir up and disturb the people. The brethren then immediately sent Paul away as far as the sea coast, while Silas and Timothy remained there. Those who conducted Paul brought him as far as Athens; and, when they had

received an order to tell Silas and Timothy to come to
him with all speed, they went away.

BEROEA was sixty miles west of Thessalonica. Three things
stand out in this short section.

(1) There is the scriptural basis of Paul's preaching. He set
the people of Beroea searching the Scriptures. The Jews were
certain that Jesus was not the Messiah because he had been
crucified. To them, anyone who had been crucified was cursed.
It was, no doubt, in passages like Isaiah 53 that Paul set the
people of Beroea to find a forecast of the work of Jesus.

(2) There is the bitterness of Jews. They not only opposed
Paul in Thessalonica; they pursued him to Beroea. The tragedy
is that undoubtedly they thought that they were doing God's
work by seeking to silence Paul. It can be a terrible thing when
people identify their aims with the will of God instead of
submitting their aims to that will.

(3) There is the courage of Paul. He had been imprisoned
in Philippi; he had left Thessalonica in peril of his life, under
cover of darkness; and once again in Beroea he had had to flee
for his life. Most people would have abandoned a struggle
which seemed bound to end in arrest and death. When the
missionary David Livingstone was asked where he was
prepared to go, he answered: 'I am prepared to go anywhere,
so long as it is forward.' The idea of turning back never
occurred to Paul either.

ALONE IN ATHENS

Acts 17:16–21

When Paul was waiting for them in Athens, his spirit
was deeply vexed as he saw the whole city full of idols.
He debated with the Jews and the worshippers in the

synagogue, and every day he talked in the city square with everyone he met. Some of the Epicurean and Stoic philosophers took issue with him. Some of them said: 'What would this gutter-sparrow of a man be saying?' Others said: 'He seems to be the herald of strange divinities.' This they said because he told the good news of Jesus and the resurrection. So they took him and brought him to the Areopagus, saying: 'May we know what is this strange new teaching you are talking about? For you are introducing things which sound strange to us. We want therefore to know what these things mean.' (All the Athenians and the strangers who stay there have no time for anything other than to talk about and to listen to the latest idea.)

WHEN he fled from Beroea, Paul found himself alone in Athens. But, whether with comrades or alone, Paul never stopped preaching Christ. Athens had long since left behind its great days of action, but it was still the greatest university town in the world, to which those seeking learning came from far and wide. It was a city of many gods. It was said that there were more statues of the gods in Athens than in all the rest of Greece put together, and that in Athens it was easier to meet a god than another person. In the great city square, people met to talk, for in Athens they did little else. Paul would have no difficulty in getting someone to talk to – and the philosophers soon discovered him.

There were the *Epicureans*. (1) They believed that everything happened by chance. (2) They believed that death was the end of everything. (3) They believed that the gods were remote from the world and did not care. (4) They believed that pleasure was the chief purpose in life. They did not mean physical and material pleasure; for the highest pleasure was that which involved no pain.

There were the *Stoics*. (1) They believed that everything was God. God was fiery spirit. That spirit grew dull in matter, but it was in everything. What gave human beings life was that a little spark of that spirit dwelt in them, and when they died it returned to God. (2) They believed that everything that happened was the will of God and therefore must be accepted without resentment. (3) They believed that every so often the world disintegrated and was burnt up and started all over again on the same cycle of events.

They took Paul to the Areopagus (the Greek for Mars' Hill). It was the name both of the hill and of the court that met on it. The court was very select, consisting of perhaps only thirty members. It dealt with cases of homicide and had the oversight of public morals. There, in the most learned city in the world and before the most exclusive of courts, Paul had to state his faith. It might have daunted anyone else; but Paul was never ashamed of the gospel of Christ. To him, this was another God-given opportunity to witness for Christ.

A SERMON TO THE PHILOSOPHERS

Acts 17:22-31

> Paul stood up in the midst of the Areopagus and said: 'Men of Athens, I see that in all things you are as superstitious as possible. As I came through your city and as I saw the objects of your worship, I found among them an altar with the inscription: "To the Unknown God." So then, what you worship and do not know, this I preach to you. God, who made the universe and everything in it, this God is Lord of heaven and earth and does not dwell in temples made with hands; nor is he served by the hands of men, as if he needed anything, but he himself gives to all life and breath and all things.

He made of one every race of men to dwell on all the
face of the earth, and he fixed the appointed times and
boundaries of their habitations. He made men so that
they might search for God, if they might perchance feel
after him and find him; and indeed he is not far from
any one of us. For by him we live and move and are. As
some of your own poets have said: "We too are his
offspring." Since, then, we are the offspring of God, we
should not think that the Divine is like gold or silver or
stone, engraved by the art and design of man. So then
God overlooked the times of ignorance; but now he gives
orders to men that all men everywhere should repent.
Thus he has fixed a day in which he will judge the world
in righteousness by a man whom he ordained for that
task, and he has given proof of this by raising him from
the dead.'

THERE were many altars to unknown gods in Athens. Some
600 years before this, a terrible plague had fallen on the city
which nothing could halt. A Cretan poet, Epimenides, had come
forward with a plan. A flock of sheep were starved and then
set loose on the Areopagus (lush with grass). It would have
been unnatural for them not to eat – and those that lay down
instead of eating were sacrificed on altars to an unknown god
which were then constructed alongside where the sheep
were lying. Many such altars were constructed, which had later
fallen into disrepair. By Paul's day, one had been restored to
its original condition. In the original story, the plague was
lifted as a result of these sacrifices. It is from this situation
that Paul takes his starting point. There are a series of steps in
his sermon.

(1) God is not the made but the maker; and the one who
made all things cannot be worshipped by anything made by
human hands. It is all too true that people often worship what

their hands have made. If our God is that to which we give all our time, thought and energy, many of us are clearly engaged in worshipping things which are of our own creation.

(2) God has guided history. He was behind the rise and fall of nations in the days gone by; his hand is on the helm of things now.

(3) God has made human beings in such a way that instinctively they long for God and search for him in the darkness.

(4) The days of feeling our way and of ignorance are past. As long as people had to search in the shadows, they could not know God, and he excused their follies and their mistakes; but now in Christ the full blaze of the knowledge of God has come, and the day of excuses is past.

(5) The day of judgment is coming. Life is neither a progress to extinction, as it was to the Epicureans, nor a pathway to absorption to God, as it was to the Stoics; it is a journey to the judgment seat of God, where Jesus Christ is Judge.

(6) The proof of the pre-eminence of Christ is the resurrection. It is no unknown God but a risen Christ with whom we have to deal.

THE REACTIONS OF THE ATHENIANS

Acts 17:32-4

> When they heard of a resurrection of dead men, some mocked and some said: 'We will hear about this again'; but some attached themselves to him and believed. Among these were Dionysius the Areopagite and a woman called Damaris, together with others.

IT would seem on the whole that Paul had less success in Athens than anywhere else. It was typical of the Athenians that all they wanted was to talk. They did not want action; they did not even particularly want conclusions. They wanted simply mental acrobatics and the stimulus of mental exercise.

There were three main reactions. (1) Some mocked. They were amused by the passionate earnestness of this strange Jew. It is possible to make light of life; but those who do so will find that what began as comedy must end in tragedy. (2) Some put off their decision. The most dangerous of all days is when we discover how easy it is to talk about tomorrow. (3) Some believed. The wise know that only the fool will reject God's offer.

Two converts are named. There is Dionysius the Areopagite. As already said, the Areopagus was composed of perhaps not more than thirty people, so that Dionysius must have been one of the intellectual aristocracy of Athens. There was Damaris. The position of women in Athens was very restricted. It is unlikely that any respectable woman would have been in the market square at all. The likelihood is that she turned from a way of shame to a way of life. Once again, we see the gospel making its appeal to all classes and conditions of men and women.

PREACHING IN CORINTH

ITS very position made Corinth a key city in Greece. Greece is almost cut in two by the sea. On one side is the Saronic Gulf with its port of Cenchrea, and on the other is the Corinthian Gulf with its port of Lechaeum. Between the two, there is an isthmus – a neck of land less than five miles across – and on that isthmus stood Corinth. All north–south traffic in Greece had to pass through Corinth, because there was no other way. The city was called 'the Bridge of Greece'. But the voyage round the southern extremity of Greece was a voyage of great peril. The southernmost cape was Cape Malea, and to round it was the equivalent of rounding Cape Horn. The Greeks had a proverb: 'Let him who thinks of sailing round Malea make his will.' Consequently the east–west trade of the Mediterranean also passed through Corinth, for many chose that way rather than the perilous voyage round Malea. Corinth was 'the market place of Greece'.

Corinth was more than a great commercial centre. It was also the home of the Isthmian Games, which were second only to the Olympic Games.

Corinth was also a wicked city. The Greeks had a verb, 'to play the Corinthian', which meant to live a life of lustful debauchery. The word 'Corinthian' came into the English language in the early decades of the nineteenth century, in Regency times, to describe reckless young men who indulged in riotous living. In Greece, if ever a Corinthian was shown on the stage, he was shown drunk. Dominating Corinth stood the hill of the Acropolis. The hill was not only a fortress; it was a temple of Aphrodite. In its great days, the temple had 1,000 priestesses of Aphrodite who were sacred prostitutes and who, at evening, came down to the city streets to ply their trade. It had become a proverb: 'Not every man can afford a journey to Corinth.'

This was the city in which Paul lived and worked and had some of his greatest triumphs. When he was writing to the Corinthians, he made a list of all kinds of wickedness. 'Do you not know that wrongdoers will not inherit the kingdom of God? Do not be deceived! Fornicators, idolators, adulterers, male prostitutes, sodomites, thieves, the greedy, drunkards, revilers, robbers – none of these will inherit the kingdom of God.' And then comes the triumphant phrase: '*and this is what some of you used to be*' (1 Corinthians 6:9–11). The very iniquity of Corinth was the opportunity of Christ.

IN THE WORST CITY OF ALL

Acts 18:1–11

> After this, Paul left Athens and came to Corinth. There
> he found a Jew called Aquila, who was a native of
> Pontus, but who had newly arrived from Italy with his
> wife Priscilla, because Claudius had decreed that all Jews
> must leave Rome. Paul went in to these people, and,
> because they had the same craft as he had, he worked
> with them; for they were leather-workers to trade. Every
> Sabbath, he debated in the synagogue and he won over
> both Jews and Greeks.
>
> When Silas and Timothy came down from
> Macedonia, Paul proceeded to devote himself entirely
> to preaching, and he kept testifying to the Jews that Jesus
> was God's Anointed One. When they opposed him and
> spoke blasphemous words, he shook out his raiment
> against them and said: 'Your blood be on your own head;
> I am clean; from now on I will go to the Gentiles.' So
> he removed from there and went to the house of a man
> called Titus Justus, who was a worshipper of God, and
> whose house was next door to the synagogue. Crispus,
> the president of the synagogue, believed in the Lord
> with all his household. And many of the Corinthians
> listened and believed and were baptized. The Lord said
> to Paul in a vision by night: 'Stop being afraid; go on
> speaking and do not be silent, because I am with you
> and no one will lay hands on you to hurt you, for
> many people are mine in this city.' He settled there for
> a year and six months, teaching the word of God among
> them.

HERE we have a vivid light on the kind of life that Paul lived.
He was a Rabbi – and, according to Jewish practice, every
Rabbi must have a trade. He must take no money for preaching

and teaching and must make his own living. The Jews glorified work. 'Love work', they said. 'He who does not teach his son a trade teaches him robbery.' 'Excellent', they said, 'is the study of the law along with a worldly trade; for the practice of them both makes a man forget iniquity; but all law without work must in the end fail and causes iniquity.' So we find Rabbis following every respectable trade. It meant that they never became detached scholars and always knew what the life of those who had to work at a trade was like.

Paul is described as a tent-maker. Tarsus was in Cilicia; in that province there were herds of a certain kind of goat with a special kind of fleece. Out of that fleece, a cloth called *cilicium* was made which was regularly used for making tents and curtains and hangings. Doubtless Paul worked at that trade, although the Greek word used means more than a tent-maker; it means a leather-worker, and Paul must have been a skilled craftsman. He was always proud of the fact that he was not a burden to anyone (1 Thessalonians 2:9; 2 Thessalonians 3:8; 2 Corinthians 11:9). But probably when Silas and Timothy arrived they brought a present, perhaps from the church at Philippi, which loved Paul so much; and that present made it possible for him to devote his whole time to preaching. It was in AD 49 that Claudius banished all the Jews from Rome, and it must have been then that Aquila and Priscilla came to Corinth.

Just when Paul needed it, God spoke to him. Often, he must have been daunted by the task that faced him in Corinth. He was a man of intense emotions, and often he must have had his times of reaction. But, when God gives us a task to do, he also gives us the power to do it. In the presence of God, Paul found his courage and his strength.

UNBIASED ROMAN JUSTICE

Acts 18:12–17

> When Gallio was proconsul of Achaia, the Jews got
> together to make an attack on Paul. They brought him
> to the judgment seat and said: 'This man seduces
> men to worship God contrary to the law.' When Paul
> was going to speak, Gallio said to the Jews: 'You
> Jews, if this were a matter of crime or of wicked mis-
> behaviour I would of course listen with patience to
> you; but if this is a question of talk and words and a
> law observed by you, see to it yourselves. I have no
> wish to be judge of these things.' So he drove them from
> his judgment seat. And they all took Sosthenes, the
> president of the synagogue, and beat him before the
> judgment seat. And Gallio took no account of these
> things.

As usual, the Jews sought to make trouble for Paul. It was
very likely that it was when Gallio first became proconsul
that the Jews attempted to get him to act against the Christians,
trying to influence him before he was settled in. Gallio was
famous for his kindness. Seneca, his brother, said of him:
'Even those who love my brother Gallio to the utmost of their
power do not love him enough', and also: 'No man was ever
as sweet to one as Gallio is to all.' The Jews sought to
take advantage of Gallio; but he was an unbiased Roman.
He was well aware that Paul and his friends were not guilty
of any crime and that the Jews were trying to use him for
their own purposes. At the side of the judgment seat were his
lictors, the court officials who were armed with their rods,
and he ordered them to drive the Jews from his judgment
seat. The Authorized Version translates the latter part of verse
17: 'Gallio cared for none of those things.' That has often

been taken to mean that Gallio was uninterested; but its real meaning is that he was absolutely fair and refused to allow himself to be influenced.

In this passage, we see the indisputable value of a Christian life. Gallio knew that no fault could be found with Paul and his friends.

THE RETURN TO ANTIOCH

Acts 18:18–23

> After Paul had remained there many days longer, he took leave of the brethren and sailed away to Syria, and Priscilla and Aquila went with him. At Cenchrea he had his head shorn, for he had a vow. They arrived at Ephesus and he left them there. He himself went into the synagogue and debated with the Jews. They asked him to stay a longer time but he would not consent to do so, but he took leave of them saying: 'God willing, I will come back to you again', and he set out from Ephesus. When he had landed at Caesarea, he went up and greeted the church and then came down to Antioch. When he had spent some time there he went away, and he went successively through the Galatian country and Phrygia, establishing all the disciples.

PAUL was on the way home. His route was by Cenchrea, the port of Corinth, and from there on to Ephesus. Then he went to Caesarea; from there he went up and greeted the church, which means that he went up to see the leaders at Jerusalem; after that he went back to Antioch, the place from which he had started.

At Cenchrea, he had his hair cut because of a vow. When a Jew particularly wanted to thank God for some blessing, he took the Nazirite vow (Numbers 6:1–21). If that vow was carried out in full, it meant that for thirty days he neither ate meat nor drank wine; and he allowed his hair to grow. At the end of the thirty days, he made certain offerings in the Temple; his hair was cut and burned on the altar as an offering to God. No doubt Paul was thinking of all God's goodness to him in Corinth and took this vow to show his gratitude.

THE THIRD MISSIONARY JOURNEY

THE story of the third missionary journey begins at Acts 18:23. It began with a tour of Galatia and Phrygia to offer strength to the disciples there. Paul then moved on to Ephesus, where he remained for nearly three years. From there, he went to Macedonia; he then crossed over to Troas and proceeded by way of Miletus, Tyre and Caesarea to Jerusalem.

THE ENTRY OF APOLLOS

Acts 18:24–8

A Jew called Apollos, who was a native of Alexandria and a man of culture, arrived in Ephesus. He was able to use the Scriptures to great effect. This man had been instructed in the Way of the Lord. He was full of enthusiasm and he told and taught the story of Jesus with accuracy, but he knew only the baptism of John. This man began to speak boldly in the synagogue. When Priscilla and Aquila heard him, they took him and more accurately explained the Way of God to him. When he wished to go over to Achaea, the brethren encouraged him and wrote to the disciples to make him welcome. When he had arrived, he was of great help to those who had believed through grace, for he vigorously confuted

the Jews in public debate, demonstrating through the
Scriptures that Jesus was the Anointed One.

CHRISTIANITY is here described as the Way of the Lord. One
of the most common titles in Acts is the Way (9:2, 19:9, 19:23,
22:4, 24:14, 24:22); and that title shows us at once that
Christianity means not only believing certain things but putting
them into practice.

Apollos came from Alexandria, where there were about
1,000,000 Jews. Their strength in numbers was so great that
two out of the five wards into which Alexandria was divided
were Jewish. Alexandria was the city of scholars. It was
especially the place where scholars believed in the allegorical
interpretation of the Old Testament. They believed that not
only did the Old Testament record history but also every
recorded event had an inner meaning. Because of this, Apollos
would be exceedingly useful in convincing the Jews, for he
would be able to find references to Christ all over the Old
Testament and to prove to them that the Old Testament looked
forward all the time to Christ's coming.

For all that, there was something lacking in his training.
He knew only the baptism of John. When we come to deal
with the next passage, we shall see more clearly what that
means. But we can say now that Apollos must have seen the
need for repentance and have recognized Jesus as the Messiah;
but as yet he did not know the good news of Jesus as the
Saviour of all people and of the coming of the Holy Spirit in
power. He knew of the task Jesus gave men and women to
do, but he did not yet fully know of the help Jesus gave them
to do it. Aquila and Priscilla gave him fuller and more accurate
instruction. The result was that Apollos, who already knew
Jesus as a figure in history, came also to know him as a living
presence; and his power as a preacher must have been
increased dramatically.

IN EPHESUS

ACTS 19 is mainly concerned with Paul's work in Ephesus. He stayed longer there than anywhere else – almost three years.

(1) Ephesus was the market of Asia Minor. In those days, trade followed the river valleys. Ephesus stood at the mouth of the Cayster and therefore commanded the richest hinterland in Asia Minor. Revelation 18:12–13 gives a description of the trade of Ephesus. It was known as 'the Treasure House of Asia' and has been called 'the Vanity Fair of Asia Minor'.

(2) It was an assize town. That is to say, at specified times, the Roman governor came there and important cases of justice were tried. The city knew the pomp and pageantry of Roman power and Roman justice.

(3) It was the location for the Pan-Ionian Games, which the whole country came to see. To be president of these games and to be responsible for their organization was a greatly coveted honour. The men who held this high office were called *Asiarchs* and are referred to in 19:31.

(4) It was the home of criminals. The Temple of Diana possessed the right of asylum. That is to say, any criminal reaching the area round the temple was safe. Inevitably, therefore, Ephesus had become the home of the criminals of the ancient world.

(5) It was a centre of superstition. It was famous for charms and spells called 'Ephesian Letters'. They were guaranteed to bring safety on a journey, to bring children to the childless, or to bring success in love or in any business enterprise. From all over the world, people came to buy these magic parchments, which they wore as lucky charms.

(6) The greatest glory of Ephesus was the Temple of Artemis. Artemis and Diana were one and the same, Artemis

being the Greek name, Diana the Latin. This temple was one
of the seven wonders of the world. It was 425 feet long by
220 feet wide by 60 feet high. There were 127 pillars, each
the gift of a king. They were all of glittering Parian marble,
and thirty-six of them were marvellously gilded and inlaid.
The great altar had been carved by Praxiteles, the greatest of
all Greek sculptors. The image of Artemis was not beautiful.
It was a black, squat, many-breasted figure, signifying fertility;
it was so old that no one knew where it had come from or
even of what material it was made. The story was that it had
fallen from heaven.

INCOMPLETE CHRISTIANITY

Acts 19:1–7

> It happened that, when Apollos was in Corinth, Paul
> went through the upper districts and came to Ephesus
> and found certain disciples there. He said to them: 'When
> you believed, did you receive the Holy Spirit?' They
> said to him: 'No, we never even heard that the Holy
> Spirit exists.' He said to them: 'With what, then, were
> you baptized?' They said: 'With the baptism of John.'
> Paul said: 'It was the baptism of repentance that John
> administered, and he told the people that it was on him
> who was to come after him that they must believe – and
> this is Jesus.' When they heard this, they were baptized
> in the name of the Lord Jesus. And when Paul laid his
> hands on them the Holy Spirit came upon them and they
> spoke with tongues and prophesied. In all there were
> about twelve of these men.

In Ephesus, Paul met some men whose Christianity was not
yet complete. They had received the baptism of John, but they
did not even know of the Holy Spirit in the Christian sense of

the term. What was the difference between the baptism of John and baptism in the name of Jesus? The accounts of the preaching of John (Matthew 3:7–12; Luke 3:3–11) reveal one fundamental difference between it and the preaching of Jesus. The preaching of John was a threat; the preaching of Jesus was good news. John's preaching was a stage on the way. He himself knew that he only pointed to one still to come (Matthew 3:11; Luke 3:16).

John's preaching was a necessary stage, because there are two stages in the religious life. First, there is the stage in which we awaken to our own inadequacy and the fact that we are deserving of condemnation at the hand of God. That stage is closely linked to an endeavour to do better that inevitably fails because we try in our own strength. Second, there is the stage when we come to see that through the grace of Jesus Christ our condemnation may be taken away. Closely linked with that stage is the time when we find that all our efforts to do better are strengthened by the work of the Holy Spirit, through whom we can do what we could never do on our own.

These Christians knew the condemnation and the moral duty of being better; but the grace of Christ and the help of the Holy Spirit they did not know. Their faith was incomplete. Their religion was inevitably a matter of struggle and had not reached the stage of being an experience of peace. The incident shows us one great truth – that without the Holy Spirit there can be no such thing as complete Christianity. Even when we see the error of our ways and repent and determine to change them, we can never make the change without the help which only the Spirit can give.

THE WORKS OF GOD

Acts 19:8–12

> He came into the synagogue and for three months he
> spoke with boldness, debating and persuading people
> about the things connected with the kingdom of God.
> When some made themselves difficult and would not
> believe, and when they spoke ill of the Way before the
> congregation, he left them and withdrew the disciples
> from them and debated daily in the hall of Tyrannus.
> This went on for two years, so that all who lived in
> Asia, Jews and Greek alike, heard the word of God;
> and God kept on doing extraordinary works of power
> through Paul's hands, so that sweat-bands and aprons
> which had touched his body were taken away to the
> sick and their diseases left them and the evil spirits
> departed.

WHEN work in the synagogue became impossible because of
the embittered opposition, Paul changed his regular meeting
place to the hall of a philosopher called Tyrannus. One Greek
manuscript adds a touch which sounds like the additional detail
an eyewitness might bring. It says that Paul taught in that hall
from 11 am to 4 pm. Almost certainly, that is when Paul would
teach. Until 11 am and after 4 pm, Tyrannus would need the
hall himself. In the Ionian cities, all work stopped at 11 am
and did not begin again until the late afternoon because of the
heat. We are told that there would actually be more people
sound asleep in Ephesus at 1 pm than at 1 am. What Paul
must have done was to work all morning and all evening at
his trade and to teach in the midday hours. It shows us two
things – the eagerness of Paul to teach and the eagerness of
the Christians to learn. The only time they had was when others
rested in the heat of the day – and they seized that time. It

may well put many of us to shame for complaining that things are inconvenient at times.

Throughout this time, wonderful deeds were being done. The sweat-band was what a workman wore round his head to absorb the sweat as he worked. The apron was the girdle which a workman or servant wrapped around himself. It is very significant that the narrative does not say that Paul did these extraordinary deeds; it says that God did them through Paul's hands. It has been said that God is everywhere looking for hands to use. We may not be able to work miracles with our hands, but without doubt we can give them to God so that he may work through them.

THE DEATH-BLOW TO SUPERSTITION

Acts 19:13–20

Some of the itinerant Jewish exorcists tried naming the name of Jesus over those who had evil spirits. They said: 'I adjure you by Jesus whom Paul preaches.' There were seven sons of a certain Scaeva, a Jewish chief priest, who did this. The evil spirit answered them: 'Jesus I know and Paul I understand, but who are you?' And the man, in whom the evil spirit was, leaped on them and mastered them all and overpowered them so that they fled naked and battered from that house. This became known to all the Jews and Greeks who lived in Ephesus; and awe fell upon all of them; and the name of the Lord Jesus was magnified. Many of those who had believed came and confessed their faith and revealed the spells which they had used. Many of those who had practised magic brought their books and burned them in the presence of all. They calculated the value of them and found that it amounted to about 50,000 silver coins. So the word of the Lord increased mightily and prevailed.

THIS is a vivid bit of local colour from the Ephesian scene. In those days, everyone believed that illness and disease, and especially mental illness, were the result of the activity of evil spirits which settled in an individual. Exorcism was a regular trade. If the exorcist knew the name of a more powerful spirit than the one which had taken up residence in the afflicted person, by speaking that name it was possible to overpower the evil spirit and make it depart. There is no reason to disbelieve that these things happened. The human mind is a strange thing, and even misguided and superstitious faith has its results in the mercy of God.

When some of the exorcists tried to use the name of Jesus, the most alarming things happened. The result was that many of the quacks, and also many of those who were sincere, saw the error of their ways. Nothing can more definitely show the reality of the change than the fact that in superstition-ridden Ephesus they were willing to burn the books and the charms which were so profitable to them. They are an example to us. They made the cleanest of clean breaks, even though it meant abandoning the things that were their livelihood. It is all too true that many of us hate our sins – but either we cannot leave them at all or we do so with a lingering and backward look. There are times when only the clean and final break will suffice.

THE PURPOSE OF PAUL

Acts 19:21-2

> When everything was completed, Paul purposed in the Spirit to go through Macedonia and go to Jerusalem.

He said: 'After I have been there, I must see Rome
too.' He sent Timothy and Erastus, two of his helpers,
into Macedonia, and he himself extended his stay in
Asia.

IT is only by the merest hint that Luke gives us an indication
here of something which is filled out in Paul's letters. He tells
us that Paul intended to go to Jerusalem. The church in
Jerusalem was poor; and Paul aimed to take a collection
from all his Gentile churches as a contribution to it. We
find references to this collection in 1 Corinthians 16:1ff.,
2 Corinthians 9:1ff. and Romans 15:25–6. Paul pressed on
with this scheme for two reasons. First, he wished in the most
practical way to emphasize the unity of the Church. He wanted
to demonstrate that they belonged to the body of Christ and
that when one part of the body suffered all must help. In other
words, he wanted to take them away from a merely congregational outlook and to give them a vision of the one universal
Church of which they were part. Second, he wanted to teach
them practical Christian charity. Doubtless when they heard
of the poverty and need of the Christians in Jerusalem they
felt sorry. He wanted to teach them that sympathy must be
translated into action. These two lessons are as valid today as
ever they were.

RIOT IN EPHESUS

Acts 19:23–41

It happened that at this time there was a great disturbance
about the Way. A certain man called Demetrius, who
was a silversmith and who made silver shrines of
Artemis, brought very considerable profit to the craftsmen. He called them together, with the workers who

were engaged in like crafts, and said: 'Men, you know that our prosperity depends on this craft; and you see and hear how not only in Ephesus but throughout nearly the whole of Asia this fellow Paul has won over and led away a great number of people telling them that gods made with hands are not gods at all. There is risk for us that not only our business may come into disrepute but also that the shrine of the great goddess Artemis may come to be held of no importance, and that she whom the whole of Asia and the civilized world worships should be robbed of her greatness.' When they heard this, they were filled with anger and they kept shouting: 'Great is Artemis of the Ephesians.' So the whole city was filled with confusion. By common consent they rushed to the theatre; and they seized Gaius and Aristarchus, who were fellow travellers of Paul's. Paul wished to go in to the people, but the disciples would not let him. Some of the Asiarchs, who were friendly to him, sent to him and urged him not to venture into the theatre. Some kept shouting one thing and some another. The meeting was confused, and the majority had no idea why it had met. At the proposal of the Jews, some of the crowd put forward Alexander. Alexander made a gesture with his hand and wished to make a defence to the people. When they realized that he was a Jew, one shout arose from them all, as for about two hours they kept crying: 'Great is Artemis of the Ephesians.' But the town secretary quietened the crowd. He said: 'Men of Ephesus, what man is there who does not know that the city of Ephesus is the temple-guardian of the great Artemis and of the image which fell from heaven? Since these things are beyond dispute, we must remain quiet and do nothing reckless. You have brought in these men who are neither temple-robbers nor blasphemers of our goddess. If Demetrius and his fellow craftsmen have a case against anyone, sessions are held and there are proconsuls. Let them bring a case against each other. If you are anxious for further steps to be taken, the matter can be settled in a properly constituted assembly. For we are running the risk of being charged with a riot for this day's events since there is no cause which we could advance as a reason for this uproar.' And with these words he dismissed the assembly.

THIS thrilling story sheds a great deal of light on the characters in it. First, there are Demetrius and the silversmiths. Their trouble was that their pockets were being affected. True, they declared that they were jealous for the honour of Artemis; but they were more worried about their incomes. When pilgrims came to Ephesus, they liked to take souvenirs home, such as the little model shrines which the silversmiths made. Christianity was making such progress that their trade was threatened.

Second, there is the man whom the Authorized and Revised Standard Versions call the 'town clerk'. He was more than that. He kept the public records; he introduced business in the assembly; correspondence to Ephesus was addressed to him. He was worried at the possibility of a riot. Rome was a kindly ruler, but the one thing it would not stand was civil disorder. If there were riots in any town, Rome would want to know the reason why, and the magistrates responsible might lose their positions. He saved Paul and his companions, but he saved them because he was saving his own skin.

Third, there is Paul. Paul wanted to face the mob, but they would not let him. Paul was a man without fear. For the silversmiths and the town clerk, it was safety first; for Paul, it was always safety last.

SETTING OUT FOR JERUSALEM

Acts 20:1–6

After the disturbance had ceased, Paul sent for the
disciples. He spoke words of encouragement to them
and bade them farewell and departed to go to Macedonia.
When he had gone through those parts and when he
had spoken many a word of encouragement to them,
he went into Greece. When he had spent three months
there, and when he was about to set sail for Syria, a plot
was made against him by the Jews. So he made up his
mind to make the return journey through Macedonia.
As far as Asia there accompanied him Sopatros, the
son of Pyrrhus, who belonged to Beroea; and, of the
Thessalonians, Aristarchus and Secundus; and Gaius
from Derbe and Timothy; and the men from Asia,
Tychichus and Trophimus. They went on ahead and
waited for us at Troas. After the days of unleavened
bread, we sailed away from Philippi; and in five days'
time we came to them at Troas; and there we spent seven
days.

WE have already seen how Paul had set his heart on making a
collection from all his churches for the church of Jerusalem.
It was to receive contributions to that fund that he went into
Macedonia. Here again we have an instance of how much we
do not know and will never know about the story of Paul.
Verse 2 says that when he had gone through those parts he
came to Greece. It must have been on this occasion that he
visited Illyricum (Romans 15:19). These few words sum-
marize what must have been something like a whole year of
journey and adventure.

Verse 3 tells us that when Paul was about to set sail from
Greece to Syria a Jewish plot was uncovered and he changed

his route to an overland way. Most probably, what happened was this. Often, Jewish pilgrim ships left from foreign ports for Syria to take pilgrims to the Passover – and Paul must have intended to sail on one. On such a ship, it would have been the easiest thing in the world for the Jews who opposed Paul to arrange that he should disappear overboard and never be heard of again. Paul was a man who always walked with his life in his hands.

In verse 4, we have a list of Paul's companions on his voyage. These men must have been delegated from the various churches charged with the duty of taking their contributions to Jerusalem. They were demonstrating at this early stage that the Church was a unity and that the need of one part was the opportunity of the rest.

In verse 5, the narrative turns from the third to the first person again. This is the sign that once again Luke is there and that we are getting an eyewitness account. Luke tells us that they left Philippi after the days of unleavened bread. The days of unleavened bread began with the day of the Passover and lasted for one week, during which the Jews ate unleavened bread in memory of their deliverance from Egypt. The time of the Passover was the middle of April.

A YOUNG MAN FALLS ASLEEP

Acts 20:7-12

> On the first day of the week, when we had gathered together to break bread, Paul, who was about to leave on the next day, spoke to them, and he prolonged his talk until midnight. There were many lamps in the upper room where we were assembled. A young man called Eutychus was sitting by the window. He began to be

overcome by a deep sleep. While Paul was talking, he was still more overcome by sleep and he fell right down from the third floor and was taken up dead. Paul went down and threw himself on him. He put his arms round him and said: 'Stop making a fuss, for his life is still in him.' So he went back upstairs and broke bread and ate; and he talked with them a long time until dawn came and so he departed. And they brought in the boy alive and were greatly comforted.

THIS vivid story is clearly an eyewitness account; and it is one of the first accounts we have of what a Christian service was like.

It talks twice about breaking of bread. In the early Church, there were two closely related things. One was what was called the Love Feast. All contributed to it, and it was a real meal – often the only proper meal that poor slaves got all week. Here, Christians ate in loving fellowship with each other. The other was the Lord's Supper, which was observed during or immediately after the Love Feast. It may well be that we have lost something of great value in the happy togetherness of the common meal. It marked as nothing else could the family spirit of the Church.

All this happened at night – probably because it was only at night, when the day's work was done, that slaves could come to the Christian fellowship. That also explains the case of Eutychus. It was dark. In the low-ceilinged upper room, it was hot. The many lamps made the air oppressive. Eutychus, no doubt, had already done a hard day's work, and his body was tired. He was sitting by a window to get the cool night air. The windows were not made of glass. They were either lattice or solid wood and opened like doors, coming right down almost to the floor and projecting over the courtyard below. Eutychus, overpowered by the stuffy atmosphere, succumbed to sleep and fell to the courtyard below. We must not take it that Paul spoke on and on; there would be talk and discussion. When the crowd poured down the outside stair and found the young man lying unconscious below, they began to scream; but Paul told them to stop the fuss, for the youth was still alive. From the next verses, we learn that Paul did not go with the main company; no doubt he stayed behind to make sure that Eutychus was completely recovered from his fall.

There is something very lovely about this simple picture. The impression is that of a family meeting together rather than of a modern church service. Is it possible that we have gained in dignity in our church services at the expense of family atmosphere?

STAGES ON THE WAY

Acts 20:13–16

> But we went to the ship and set sail for Assos, for there we intended to take Paul on board for he had arranged things in this way, since he himself intended to do that stage on foot. When we met him at Assos, we took him on board and went to Mitylene. On the next day, we sailed away from there and arrived opposite Chios. On the second day we crossed over to Samos, and on the next day we came to Miletus, for Paul had decided to sail past Ephesus so as not to have to spend time in Asia. For he was in a hurry to be, if it were possible for him, in Jerusalem on the day of Pentecost.

BECAUSE Luke was with Paul, we can follow the journey almost day by day and stage by stage. From Troas, Assos was twenty miles by road whereas it was thirty miles by sea; and the sea journey involved the rounding of Cape Lectum against the strong prevailing north-easterly winds. Paul had ample time to make the journey on foot and be picked up at Assos. It may be that he wanted the time alone in order to gather inner strength for the days ahead. Mitylene was on the island of Lesbos, Chios was on Samos, and Miletus was twenty-eight miles south of Ephesus at the mouth of the Maeander River.

We have seen how Paul would have liked to have been in Jerusalem for the Passover and how the plot of the Jews hindered that. Pentecost came seven weeks later, and he was eager to be there for that great feast. Although Paul had broken away from the Jews, the traditional Jewish feasts were still dear to him. He was the apostle to the Gentiles, and his own people might hate him; but in his heart there was nothing but love for them.

A SAD FAREWELL

Acts 20:17–38

> From Miletus, Paul sent to Ephesus and summoned the elders of the church. When they were with him, he said to them: 'You yourselves know how, from the first day I came into Asia, I spent all the time, during which I was with you, serving the Lord with all humility and with tears and amid the trials that happened to me because of the machinations of the Jews. You know how I kept back nothing that was to your profit, how I did not fail to announce my tidings to you and to teach you both publicly and from house to house, testifying to both Jews and Greeks repentance towards God and faith in our Lord Jesus Christ. And now, look you, I go bound in the Spirit to Jerusalem, although I do not know what will happen to me there, except that from city to city the Holy Spirit testifies to me that bonds and afflictions await

me. But I reckon my life worth nothing and I do not count it precious to myself, so be it that I may finish my course and complete the task I received from the Lord Jesus – the task of bearing witness of the good news of God. And now, look you, I know that all of you, among whom I went about preaching the kingdom, will see my face no more. Therefore I affirm to you this day that I am clean from the blood of all men; for I kept back nothing in my proclaiming to you of the whole will of God. Take heed for yourselves and take heed for all the flock in which the Spirit of God has appointed you overseers, so that you may be shepherds to the Church of God, which he has rescued through the blood of his own One. I know that after I have gone away fierce wolves will enter in to you and will not spare the flock; and from your own number there will arise men who will speak perverse things to draw the disciples away after them. Therefore be watchful and remember that for three years, day and night, I never stopped instructing each one of you with tears. And now I hand you over to God and to the word of his grace, which is able to build you up, and to give you an inheritance among all those who have been sanctified. I coveted no man's silver or gold or raiment. You yourselves know that these very hands served my own needs and the needs of those who were with me. Always I showed you that working like this a man must help those who are in trouble and that you must remember the words of the Lord Jesus, that it was he who said: "It is happier rather to give than to get." '

When he had said this, he knelt down and prayed with them all. And there was great lamentation among them all. They fell upon Paul's neck and kissed him repeatedly, for they were grieved most of all at the word that he had said, that they would see his face no more. And they escorted him to the ship.

It is not possible to make a neat analysis of a farewell speech so charged with emotion as this. But a number of things stand out.

First of all, Paul makes certain claims for himself.

(1) He had *spoken fearlessly*. He had told them all God's will and pandered neither to the fear nor the favour of anyone.

(2) He had *lived independently*. His own hands had supplied his needs, and his work had been not only for his own sake but also for the sake of others who were less fortunate than himself.

(3) He had *faced the future gallantly*. He was the captive of the Holy Spirit, and in that confidence he was able to face everything the future might hold.

Paul also urges certain claims upon his friends. (1) He reminded them of *their duty*. They were overseers of the flock of God. That was not a duty they had chosen but a duty for which they had been chosen. The servants of the Good Shepherd must also be shepherds of the sheep. (2) He reminded them of *their danger*. The contamination of the world is never far away. Where truth is, falsehood is bound to attack. There was a constant warfare ahead to keep the faith intact and the Church pure.

Through this entire scene runs the dominant feeling of an affection as deep as the heart itself. That feeling should be in every church; for, when love dies in any church, the work of Christ will inevitably wither.

NO RETREAT

Acts 21:1–16

> When we had torn ourselves away from them and had set sail, we sailed a straight course and came to Cos; on

the next day we reached Rhodes; and from there we came to Patara. There we found a ship which was sailing across to Phoenicia, and we embarked on her and set sail. After we had sighted Cyprus and had left it behind on the left-hand side, we sailed on to Syria and came down to Tyre, for there the ship was to discharge her cargo. We sought out the disciples, and we stayed there for seven days. They told Paul through the Holy Spirit to give up his journey to Jerusalem. When we had completed the days, we left and proceeded on our journey, while they all, with their wives and children, escorted us outside the city. We knelt down on the shore and prayed and bade each other farewell. Then we embarked on the ship and they returned home. We continued our voyage and arrived at Ptolemais from Tyre, and when we had greeted the brethren we stayed among them for one day. On the next day we left and came to Caesarea. We went into the house of Philip the evangelist, who was one of the Seven, and stayed with him. He had four daughters who were virgins and who prophesied. While we stayed there longer, a prophet called Agabus came down from Judaea. He visited us and he took Paul's girdle and he bound his own hands and feet and said: 'Thus speaks the Holy Spirit. The Jews in Jerusalem will bind the man to whom this girdle belongs like this and they will hand him over to the Gentiles.' When we heard this, both we and the people of the place kept pleading with Paul not to go to Jerusalem. Then Paul answered: 'What are you doing, weeping and breaking my heart? For I am ready not only to be bound but to die in Jerusalem for the sake of the name of the Lord Jesus.' Since he would not be persuaded, we held our peace and said: 'Let the Lord's will be done.' After these days, when we had packed up, we set out on the journey to Jerusalem. Some of the disciples from Caesarea went with us. They were to bring

us to Mnason, a man of Cyprus, an original disciple, with
whom we were to lodge.

THE narrative is speeding up, and there is an atmosphere of
approaching storm as Paul comes nearer Jerusalem. Two
things stand out here. (1) There is the sheer determination of
Paul to go on no matter what lay ahead. Nothing could have
been more definite than the warning of the disciples at Tyre
and of Agabus at Caesarea, but nothing could deter Paul from
the course that he had chosen. During one of the sieges in the
Spanish Civil War, some in the garrison wanted to surrender,
but one of their comrades said: 'I would rather die on my feet
than live on my knees.' Paul was like that. (2) There is the
wonderful fact that wherever Paul went he found a Christian
community waiting to welcome him. If that was true in Paul's
time, it is still more true today. One of the great privileges of
belonging to the Church is the fact that, no matter where we
go, we are sure to find a community of like-minded people
into which we may enter. Those who are in the family of the
Church have friends all over the world.

Agabus is an interesting figure. Jewish prophets had a
certain custom. When words were inadequate, they dramatized
their message. There are many instances of this in the Old
Testament (for example, Isaiah 20:3–4; Jeremiah 13:1–11,
27:2; Ezekiel 4, 5:1–4; 1 Kings 11:29–31).

In the Authorized Version, the antiquity of the language
may be misleading. Verse 15 says: 'We took up our carriages
and went up to Jerusalem.' That may sound as if Paul and his
friends travelled by carriage. But in the sixteenth century,
used like this, *carriage* meant not something which carried
people but something which people had to carry; it meant
baggage.

COMPROMISE IN JERUSALEM

Acts 21:17–26

> When we arrived in Jerusalem, the brethren received us
> gladly. On the next day, Paul along with us went to visit
> James; and all the elders were present. He greeted them
> and recounted one by one the things which God had
> done among the Gentiles through his ministry. When
> they heard the story, they glorified God. They said to
> him: 'You see, brother, how many thousands there are
> among the Jews who have accepted the faith. Now they
> are all devotees of the law. They have heard rumours
> about you which allege that you teach all the Jews who
> live in Gentile territory to abandon the law of Moses
> and to stop circumcising their children and to stop
> living according to their ancestral customs. What then
> is to be done? They will be bound to hear that you have
> arrived. So you must do what we tell you. We have four
> men who have taken a vow upon themselves. Take these
> men and be purified along with them; and pay their
> expenses that they may shave their heads, and then
> everyone will know that the rumours they have heard
> about you have no truth in them but that you yourself
> also walk in observance of the law. As for the Gentiles
> who have accepted the faith, we wrote decreeing that
> they should abstain from things offered to idols, from
> blood, from anything that has been strangled and from
> fornication.' Then on the next day Paul took the men
> and was purified along with them; he went into the
> Temple and announced his intention of completing the
> days of purification until the offering was made for each
> one of them.

WHEN Paul arrived in Jerusalem, he presented the church with
a problem. The leaders accepted him and saw God's hand in

his work; but rumours had been spread that he had encouraged Jews to forsake their ancestral faith. This Paul had never done. True, he had insisted that the Jewish law was irrelevant for Gentiles; but he had never sought to draw Jews away from the customs of their ancestors.

The leaders saw a way in which Paul could guarantee the orthodoxy of his own conduct. Four men were in the middle of observing the Nazirite vow. This was a vow taken in gratitude for some special blessing from the hand of God. It involved abstention from meat and wine for thirty days, during which the hair had to be allowed to grow. It seems that sometimes at least the last seven days had to be spent entirely in the Temple courts. At the end, certain offerings had to be brought – a year-old lamb for a sin offering, a ram for a peace offering, a basket of unleavened bread, cakes of fine flour mixed with oil and a meat offering and a drink offering. Finally, the hair had to be cut and burned on the altar with the sacrifice. It is obvious that this was a costly business. Work had to be given up, and all the elements of the sacrifice had to be bought. It was quite beyond the resources of many who would have wanted to undertake it. So it was considered an act of piety for some wealthier person to cover the expenses of someone taking the vow. That was what Paul was asked to do in the case of these four men – and he agreed. By so doing, he could demonstrate for all to see that he was himself an observer of the law.

There can be no doubt that the matter was distasteful to Paul. For him, the relevance of things like that had gone. But it is the sign of all who are truly great that they can subordinate their own wishes and views for the sake of the Church. There is a time when compromise is a sign not of weakness but of strength.

A SLANDEROUS CHARGE

Acts 21:27–36

> When the seven days were nearly completed and when
> the Jews from Asia had seen Paul in the Temple, they
> stirred up the whole mob and they attacked him shouting:
> 'Help, men of Israel! This is the man who teaches all
> men everywhere against the people, against the law and
> against this place. Furthermore he has brought Greeks
> into the Temple and defiled this holy place.' For they
> had seen Trophimus the Ephesian with him in the city,
> and they thought that Paul had taken him into the
> Temple. The whole city was disturbed, and the people
> rushed together. They laid hands on Paul and dragged
> him outside the Temple, and immediately the doors
> were shut. While they were trying to kill him, the
> report reached the commander of the battalion that all
> Jerusalem was in an uproar. He at once took soldiers
> and centurions and ran down to them. When they saw
> the commander and the soldiers, they stopped beating
> Paul. Then the commander came up to him and arrested
> him and ordered him to be bound with two chains. He
> asked who he was and what he had done. In the crowd,
> some shouted one thing and some another. When the
> commander was unable to discover the truth of the matter
> because of the disturbance, he ordered him to be taken
> into the barracks. When Paul came to the steps, he had
> to be carried by the soldiers because of the violence of
> the mob. For the mass of the people were following,
> shouting: 'Kill him!'

IT so happened that Paul's compromise led to disaster. It was
the time of Pentecost. Jews were present in Jerusalem from
all over the world, and certain Jews from Asia were there,
who no doubt knew how effective Paul's work in Asia had

been. They had seen Paul in the city with Trophimus, whom they most probably knew. The business of the vow had taken Paul frequently into the Temple courts, and these Asian Jews assumed that Paul had taken Trophimus into the Temple along with him.

Trophimus was a Gentile, and for a Gentile to enter the Temple was a terrible thing. Gentiles could enter the Court of the Gentiles; but between that court and the Court of the Women there was a barrier, and into that barrier there were inset tablets with this inscription: 'No man of alien race is to enter within the balustrade and fence that goes round the Temple, and if anyone is taken in the act, let him know that he has himself to blame for the penalty of death that follows.' Even the Romans took this so seriously that they allowed the Jews to carry out the death penalty for this crime.

The Asian Jews accused Paul of destroying the law, insulting the chosen people and defiling the Temple. They initiated a movement to lynch him. In the north-west corner of the Temple area stood the Castle of Antonia, built by Herod the Great. At the great festivals, when the atmosphere was electric, it was garrisoned by a cohort of 1,000 men. Rome insisted on civil order, and a riot was an unforgivable sin both for those who staged it and for the commander who allowed it. The commander heard what was going on and came down with his troops. For his own sake, Paul was arrested and chained by each arm to two soldiers. In the confusion, the commander was able to extract no coherent charge from the excited mob, and Paul was actually carried through the seething crowd into the barracks. There was never a time when Paul was nearer death than this – and it was the unbiased justice of Rome which saved his life.

FACING THE FURY OF THE MOB

Acts 21:37–40

> When Paul was about to be brought into the barracks,
> he said to the commander: 'May I say something to you?'
> He said: 'Can you speak Greek? Are you not then the
> Egyptian who some time ago started a revolution and
> led 4,000 men of the dagger-bearers out into the desert?'
> Paul said: 'I am a man who is a Jew, a native of Tarsus,
> a citizen of no mean city. I ask you, let me speak to the
> people.' When he had given his permission to do so,
> Paul stood on the steps and made a gesture with his hand
> to the people. When a great silence had fallen, he spoke
> to them in the Hebrew tongue.

THE Castle of Antonia was connected to the outer courts of
the Temple by two flights of stairs on the northern and the
western sides. As the soldiers were struggling towards the
steps to reach the sanctuary of their own barracks, Paul made
an amazing request. He asked the captain if he could be
allowed to address the furious mob. Here is Paul exercising
his consistent policy of looking his accusers in the face.

The captain was amazed to hear a cultured Greek accent
coming from this man whom the crowd were out to lynch.
Somewhere about AD 54, an Egyptian had led a band of
desperate men out to the Mount of Olives with a promise that
he could make the walls of the city fall down in front of him.
The Romans had dealt swiftly and efficiently with his
followers; but he himself had escaped, and the captain had
thought that Paul was this revolutionary Egyptian come back.

His followers had been dagger-bearers, violent nationalists
who were deliberate assassins. They concealed daggers in their
cloaks, mixed with the crowd and struck whenever they could.
But when Paul stated his credentials, the captain knew that,

whatever else Paul was, he was no revolutionary thug; and so he allowed him to speak. When Paul turned to speak, he made a gesture for silence – and, almost miraculously, complete silence fell on that roaring mob. Nothing in all the New Testament so shows the force of Paul's personality as this silence that he commanded from the mob who would have lynched him. At that moment, the very power of God flowed through him.

THE DEFENCE OF EXPERIENCE

Acts 22:1–10

'Men, brethren and fathers, listen to the defence which I now make to you.' When they heard that he was addressing them in the Hebrew language, they gave him still more quietness. So he said: 'I am a Jew; I was born in Tarsus; I was brought up in this city; I was thoroughly trained at the feet of Gamaliel in the law of our fathers; I was zealous for God, just as you all are today. I persecuted this Way to death, fettering both men and women and delivering them to prison, as the high priest and the body of the elders bear me witness. I received letters from them and I went to the brethren at Damascus, to bring those who were there in chains to Jerusalem that they might be punished. As I was on my way, when I was coming near Damascus, about midday, suddenly it happened to me that a great light from heaven shone around me. I fell to the ground and I heard a voice saying to me: "Saul, Saul, why are you persecuting me?" I answered: "Who are you, sir?" And the voice said to me: "I am Jesus of Nazareth whom you are persecuting." Those who were with me saw the light, but they did not hear the voice of the person who was speaking to me. I said: "What am I to do, Lord?" The Lord said to me:

> "Stand up and go to Damascus, and there you will be
> told about all the things that have been assigned to you
> to do." '

PAUL's defence to the mob who are out for his blood is not to
argue but to relate a personal experience; and a personal
experience is the most unanswerable argument on earth. This
defence is in essence a paradox. It stresses two things.

(1) It stresses Paul's identity with the people to whom he
is speaking. He was a Jew, and that was something he never
forgot (cf. 2 Corinthians 11:22; Philippians 3:4–5). He was a
man of Tarsus, and Tarsus was what might be called 'no mean
city'. It was one of the great ports of the Mediterranean,
standing at the mouth of the River Cydnus and being the
terminus of a road which came all across Asia Minor from
the far-off Euphrates. It was one of the greatest university
cities of the ancient world. What is more, Paul was a Rabbi,
trained at the feet of Gamaliel, who had been 'the glory of the
law' and who had died only about five years before. He had
been a persecutor in his zeal for the ancestral ways. On all
these points, Paul was entirely at one with the audience to
which he was speaking.

(2) It stresses the difference between Paul and his audience.
The fundamental difference was that he saw Christ as the
Saviour of all and God as the one who loves all people. His
audience saw God as the one who loved only the Jews. They
sought to keep the privileges of God to themselves and
regarded anyone who would widen this circle of privilege as
a blasphemer. The difference was that Paul had met Christ
face to face.

In one sense, Paul was identified with those to whom he
spoke; in another, he was separated from them. It is like that
with every Christian. As Christians, we live in the world; but
God has separated us and consecrated us to a special task.

PAUL CONTINUES HIS LIFE STORY

Acts 22:11-21

'Because I was not able to see because of the glory of that light, I came into Damascus led by the hand by those who were with me. And Ananias, a pious man as regards the law, a man to whose character all the Jews who live there bear witness, came to me and stood beside me and said: "Brother Saul, receive your sight again"; and I, in that same hour, recovered my sight, and looked up at him. He said: "The God of our fathers has chosen you to know his will, to see the Just One and to hear the voice of his mouth, because you will be a witness for him to all men of the things you have seen and heard. And now why do you wait? Rise; be baptized; and wash away your sins, calling upon his name." When I had returned to Jerusalem, and when I was praying in the Temple, it so happened that I was in a trance and I heard him saying to me: "Hurry; depart speedily from Jerusalem because they will not receive your testimony about me." And I said: "Lord, they know that it was I who, throughout the synagogues, used to throw into prison and scourge those who believe in you; and when the blood of Stephen, your witness, was shed, I too was standing by and I was agreeing to it all; and I was guarding the clothes of those who were killing him." And he said to me: "Get on your way, for I will send you far off to the Gentiles."'

ONCE again from the beginning, Paul is stressing his identity with his audience. When he reached Damascus, the man who instructed him was Ananias, a follower of the law, whom the Jews knew to be a good man. Paul is stressing the fact that he had come not to destroy the ancestral faith but to fulfil it. Here we have one of Luke's telescoped narratives. When we also read Acts 9 and Galatians 1, we find that it was really three years afterwards that Paul went up to Jerusalem, after his visit to Arabia and his witnessing in Damascus.

In Acts 9, we were told that he left Jerusalem because he was in danger of his life from the enraged Jews; here we are told he left because of a vision. There is no real contradiction; it is the same story told from different points of view. The point Paul makes is that he did not want to leave the Jews. When God told him to do so, Paul argued. He said that his previous record would be bound to make his change all the more impressive to the Jews; but God said that the Jews would never listen to him and he must go to the Gentiles.

There is a certain sense of disappointed longing here. As with his Master, Paul's own people would not receive him (John 1:11). He is literally saying: 'I had a priceless gift for you, but you would not take it; so it was offered to the Gentiles.'

Verse 14 is a summary not only of the life of Paul but also of the Christian life. There are three items in it. (1) *To know the will of God.* It is the first aim of every Christian to know God's will and to obey it. (2) *To see the Just One.* It is the aim of every Christian each day to walk in the presence of the risen Lord. (3) *To hear God's voice.* We have already noted that it was said of John Brown of Haddington that, in his preaching, he paused from time to time as if listening for a voice. Christians are always listening for the voice of God above the noise of the many voices of the world to tell them where to go and what to do.

THE EMBITTERED OPPOSITION

Acts 22:22–30

> Up to this statement they listened to him, and then they cried: 'Destroy such a fellow from the earth, for it is not

proper for him to live.' While they were shouting and
waving their garments and throwing dust into the air,
the commander ordered him to be brought into the
barracks. He ordered him to be examined by scourging
to find out why they shouted like this against him.
And when they had tied him up with the thongs, Paul
said to the centurion who was standing by: 'Is it right
for you to scourge a man who is a Roman citizen and
uncondemned?' When the centurion heard this, he
went to the commander and reported it. He said: 'What
are you going to do? This man is a Roman citizen.' The
commander came to him and said: 'Are you a Roman
citizen?' He said: 'Yes.' The commander answered: 'I
obtained this citizenship at a great price.' But Paul said:
'I was born a citizen.' So at once the men who had been
about to examine him stood away from him; and the
commander was afraid when he realized that he was a
Roman citizen and that he had fettered him. On the next
day, wishing to know the truth about the accusation made
by the Jews, he released him and ordered the chief priests
and the whole Sanhedrin to assemble; and he brought
Paul down and set him before them.

IT was the mention of Gentiles which inflamed the mob again.
It was not that the Jews objected to the preaching to the
Gentiles; what they objected to was that the Gentiles were
being offered privileges before they first accepted circumcision and the law. If Paul had preached the restricting
demands of Judaism to the Gentiles, all would have been well;
it was because he preached the grace of Christianity to them
that the Jews were enraged. They showed their disapproval
in the traditional way: they shouted and waved their garments
and threw dust in the air.

The commander did not understand Aramaic and did not
know what Paul had said; but one thing he did understand –

he must not allow a riot and must deal at once with anyone likely to cause a riot. So he decided to question Paul under scourging. This was not a punishment; it was simply the most effective way of extracting either the truth or a confession. The scourge was a leather whip studded at intervals with sharp pieces of bone and lead. Few survived it in their right senses, and many died under it.

Then Paul spoke. The Roman statesman Cicero had said: 'It is a misdeed for a Roman citizen to be bound; it is a crime for him to be beaten; it is almost as bad as to murder a father to kill him.' So Paul stated that he was a citizen. The commander was terrified. Not only was Paul a citizen; he was born free, whereas the commander had had to purchase his freedom. The commander knew that he had been on the verge of doing something which would have involved certainly his dismissal and very probably his execution. So he released Paul and determined to bring him before the Sanhedrin in order to get to the bottom of this trouble.

There were times when Paul was ready to stand on his dignity; but it was never for his own sake. He knew his task was not yet completed; gladly he would one day die for Christ; but he was too wise a man to throw his life away just yet.

PAUL'S STRATEGY

Acts 23:1–10

> Paul fixed his gaze on the Sanhedrin and said: 'Brethren, I have lived before God with a completely pure conscience up to this day.' The high priest Ananias ordered those who stood by him to strike him on the mouth. Paul said to him: 'God is going to strike you, you

whitewashed wall! Do you sit judging me according to
the law, and do you order me to be struck and so break
the law?' Those who were standing beside him said:
'Are you insulting God's high priest?' Paul said: 'I did
not know, brethren, that he was the high priest. If I had
known, I would not have spoken so, for it stands written:
"You must not speak evil of a ruler of your people."'
Now Paul knew that one section of them were Sadducees
and the other section were Pharisees, so he shouted out
in the Sanhedrin: 'Brethren, I am a Pharisee and the
son of Pharisees, and I am on trial for the hope of the
resurrection of the dead.' When he said this, a disturbance arose between the Pharisees and the Sadducees,
and the meeting was divided. For the Sadducees say that
there is no resurrection nor angel nor spirit, while the
Pharisees acknowledge both. There was a great uproar;
and some of the scribes who belonged to the party of
the Pharisees stood up and argued and said: 'We find no
fault in this man. What if a spirit or angel has spoken to
him?' When a great disturbance was going on, the
commander was so afraid that Paul might be torn apart
by them that he ordered the guard to go down and to
snatch him out of their midst and to bring him into the
barracks.

THERE was a certain audacious recklessness about Paul's
conduct before the Sanhedrin; he acted like a man who knew
that he was burning his boats. Even the way he began was a
challenge. To refer to the Sanhedrin as brothers was to put
himself on an equal footing with the court; for the normal
beginning when addressing the Sanhedrin was: 'Rulers of the
people and elders of Israel'. When the high priest ordered
Paul to be struck, he himself was breaking the law, which
said: 'Whoever strikes the cheek of an Israelite strikes, as it
were, the glory of God.' So Paul turns on him, calling him a

whitewashed wall. To touch a dead body was for an Israelite to incur ceremonial defilement; it was therefore the custom to whitewash tombs so that they might not be touched by mistake. So Paul is in effect calling the high priest a white-washed tomb.

It was indeed a crime to speak evil of a ruler of the people (Exodus 22:28). Paul knew perfectly well that Ananias was the high priest. But Ananias was notorious as a glutton, a thief, a robber and a collaborator in the Roman service. Paul's answer really means: 'That man sitting there – I never knew a man like that could be high priest of Israel.' Then Paul made a claim that he knew would make the Sanhedrin sit up. In the Sanhedrin there were Pharisees and Sadducees, whose beliefs were often opposed. The Pharisees believed in the minute details of the oral law; the Sadducees accepted only the written law. The Pharisees believed in predestination; the Sadducees believed in free will. The Pharisees believed in angels and spirits; the Sadducees did not. Above all, the Pharisees believed in the resurrection of the dead; the Sadducees did not.

So Paul claimed to be a Pharisee and that it was for the hope of resurrection from the dead that he was on trial. As a result, the Sanhedrin was split in two; and, in the violent argument that followed, Paul was nearly torn to pieces. To save him from violence, the commander had to take him back to the barracks again.

A PLOT UNCOVERED

Acts 23:11–24

> On the next night, the Lord stood by Paul and said: 'Courage! As you have testified for me in Jerusalem, so

you must bear witness in Rome also.' When it was day, the Jews formed a plot and laid themselves under a vow neither to eat nor drink until they had killed Paul. There were more than forty who formed this conspiracy. They went to the chief priests and the elders and said: 'We have laid ourselves under a vow to taste nothing until we have killed Paul. Now, therefore, do you lay information with the commander, so that he may bring him down to us, as if you were going to investigate his case more thoroughly; and we are ready to kill him before he gets as far as you.' But Paul's sister's son was there and heard the plot. So he went into the barracks and reported it to Paul. Paul called one of the centurions and said: 'Take this young man to the commander, for he has something to report to him.' He took him and brought him to the commander and said: 'The prisoner Paul called me and asked me to take this young man to you because he has something to say to you.' The commander took him by the hand and took him aside privately and asked him: 'What is it that you have to report to me?' He said: 'The Jews have got together to ask you to bring Paul down to the Sanhedrin tomorrow, as if they were going to make a more thorough investigation into his case. Do not you therefore agree to them – for more than forty, who have taken a vow upon themselves neither to eat or drink till they have killed him, are lying in wait for him; and they are now ready, expecting your assent.' The commander dismissed the young man with instructions to tell no one that – as he said – 'you have brought this information to me'. He called two of his centurions and said to them: 'Get ready 200 soldiers, 70 cavalry and 200 spearsmen to go to Caesarea at about 9 am. Provide baggage animals that they may mount Paul and get him through to Felix, the governor, in safety.'

HERE we see two things. First, we see the lengths to which the Jews would go to eliminate Paul. Under certain circumstances, the Jews regarded murder as justifiable. If people were a public danger to morals and to life, they regarded it as legitimate to eliminate them. So forty men put themselves under a vow. The vow was called a *cherem*. When a man took such a vow, he said: 'May God curse me if I fail to do this.' These men vowed neither to eat nor drink until they had assassinated Paul. Fortunately, their plan was uncovered by Paul's nephew. Second, we see the lengths to which the Roman government would go in order to administer impartial justice. Paul was a prisoner; but he was a Roman citizen, and therefore the commander mobilized a small army to see him taken in safety to Caesarea to be tried by the governor, Felix. It is strange how the hatred of the Jews – God's chosen people – contrasts with the impartial justice of the commander – a Gentile in Jewish eyes.

THE CAPTAIN'S LETTER

Acts 23:25–35

> The commander wrote a letter to the following effect: 'Claudius Lysias to his excellency Felix, the governor – greetings! When this man was seized by the Jews and when he was going to be murdered by them, I stepped in with the guard and rescued him, for I learned that he was a Roman citizen. As I wished to discover the charges on which they accused him, I brought him down to their Sanhedrin. I found that he was accused of some questions of their law and was under no charge deserving of death or bonds. When it was disclosed to me that there would be a plot against the man, I immediately sent him to you and I ordered his accusers to make their statement against him before you.'

The soldiers, according to their instructions, took Paul up and brought him by night to Antipatris. On the next day, they returned to barracks, leaving the cavalry to proceed with him. They came into Caesarea and delivered the letter to the governor and set Paul before him. When he had read the letter and had asked from what province he came, and when he had found out that he was from Cilicia, he said: 'I will hear your case when your accusers are here also'; and he ordered him to be kept in Herod's praetorium.

THE centre of Roman government was not in Jerusalem but in Caesarea. The praetorium is the residence of a governor; and the praetorium in Caesarea was a palace which had been built by Herod the Great. Claudius Lysias wrote his letter, absolutely fair and completely impartial, and the party set out. It was sixty miles from Jerusalem to Caesarea, and Antipatris was twenty-five miles from Caesarea. Up to Antipatris, the country was dangerous and inhabited by Jews; after that, the country was open and flat, quite unsuited for any ambush and largely inhabited by Gentiles. So at Antipatris the main body of the troops went back and left the cavalry alone as a sufficient escort.

The governor to whom Paul was taken was Felix, and he was famous. For five years he had governed Judaea, and for two years before that he had been stationed in Samaria; he still had two years to go before being dismissed from his post. He had begun life as a slave. His brother, Pallas, was the favourite of Nero. Through the influence of Pallas, Felix had risen first to be a freedman and then to be a governor. He was the first slave in history ever to become the governor of a Roman province. Tacitus, the Roman historian, said of him: 'He exercised the prerogatives of a king with the spirit of a slave.' He had actually been married to three princesses one

after another. The name of the first is not known; the second
was a granddaughter of Antony and Cleopatra; the third was
Drusilla, the daughter of Herod Agrippa I. He was completely
unscrupulous and was capable of hiring thugs to murder his
own closest supporters. It was to face a man like that that
Paul went to Caesarea.

A FLATTERING SPEECH
AND A FALSE CHARGE

Acts 24:1–9

> Five days afterwards, Ananias the high priest came down
> with some of the elders and with a pleader called
> Tertullus. They laid information against Paul before the
> governor. When Paul was called, Tertullus began to
> accuse him in these terms: 'Since through you we enjoy
> much tranquillity and since through your foresight many
> reforms have been brought about for this nation in every
> place and in every way, Felix, your excellency, we
> welcome it all with gratitude. But not to trouble you
> any longer, I ask you in your kindness briefly to hear
> us. When we had found this fellow a pest, a man who
> fomented disturbances among all the Jews throughout
> the civilized world, a man who is the ringleader of the
> sect of the Nazarenes – and he tried to defile the Temple,
> too – we arrested him. By examining him yourself, you
> can learn from him the charges of which we accuse him';
> and the Jews agreed with him, alleging that the facts
> were as stated.

Tertullus began his speech with a passage of almost
nauseating flattery, every word of which he and Felix knew
was quite untrue. He went on to state things which were
equally untrue. He claimed that the Jews had arrested Paul.

The scene in the Temple court was far closer to being a lynching than an arrest. The charge he levelled against Paul was subtly inaccurate; it was made up of three points.

(1) Paul was a stirrer, always in trouble and a pest. That classed Paul with those agitators who continually inflamed the easily excited populace into rebellion. Tertullus knew very well that the one thing that tolerant Rome would not stand was civil disorder – for any spark might become a flame. Tertullus knew it was a lie; but it was an effective charge.

(2) Paul was a leader of the sect of the Nazarenes. That coupled Paul with messianic movements; and the Romans knew what havoc false messiahs could cause and how they could whip the people into hysterical risings which were only settled at the cost of blood. Rome could not afford to disregard a charge like that. Again, Tertullus knew it was a lie; but it was an effective charge.

(3) Paul was a defiler of the Temple. The priests were Sadducees, the collaborationist party; to defile the Temple was to infringe the rights and laws of the priests; and the Romans, Tertullus hoped, would take the side of the pro-Roman party. The charge was that most dangerous of things – a series of half-truths and of twisted facts.

PAUL'S DEFENCE

Acts 24:10–21

When the governor had given him the sign to speak, Paul answered: 'In the knowledge that you for many years have been a judge of this people, I confidently offer my defence of my case, for you can ascertain that it is no more than twelve days since I came up to Jerusalem to worship. Neither in the Temple nor in the synagogues nor throughout the city did they find me arguing with anyone or collecting a crowd; nor can they provide any truth of the accusations which they make against me. This I do admit to you – that, according to the Way, which they call a sect, I worship my ancestral God. At the same time, I believe in all things that are written throughout the law and in the prophets, and I have the same hope towards God as they themselves accept – I mean that there will be a resurrection of the just and the unjust. Because of this, I too train myself that I may always have an unharmed conscience towards God and towards men. After many years, I came to bring alms and offerings to my people. In the course of these offerings, they found me purified in the Temple, not with a crowd and not the centre of any disturbance. But some Jews from Asia – who ought to be present before you and who ought to be bringing whatever accusation they had against me – or let they themselves say what offence they found in me as I stood before the Sanhedrin, other than in regard to this one expression I used as I stood among them – "Concerning the resurrection of the dead I am on trial today before you."'

BEGINNING at the passage 'But some Jews from Asia . . .', Paul's grammar went wrong. He began to say one thing and in mid-flow changed over to another so that the sentence became quite disconnected. But its very disconnection shows vividly the excitement and tension of the scene. Paul's defence is that of someone whose conscience is clear – it is simply to state the facts. The tragedy is that it was when he was bringing the contributions from his churches for the poor of Jerusalem and when he was meticulously observing the Jewish law that arrest came. One of the greatest things about Paul is that he speaks in his own defence with force and sometimes with a flash of indignation, but never with the self-pity or bitterness that would have been so natural in one whose finest actions had been so cruelly and deliberately misinterpreted.

PLAIN SPEAKING TO A GUILTY GOVERNOR

Acts 24:22–7

> But Felix, who had a very good knowledge of the facts about the Way, put them off, saying: 'When Lysias the commander comes down, I will go into your case.' He instructed the centurion that Paul was to be held under guard, that he was to be allowed some freedom, and he instructed him not to hinder any of his friends from rendering him service. Some days after, Felix came with his wife Drusilla, who was a Jewess, and sent for Paul and listened to him about the faith in Christ Jesus. While Paul talked about righteousness, self-control and judgment to come, Felix was afraid and said: 'For the present, go your way. When I have time I will send for you.' At the same time, he hoped that money would be given him by Paul, so he sent for him quite often and used to have conversation with him. At the end of two years, Felix was succeeded by Porcius Festus; but Felix, wishing to ingratiate himself with the Jews, left Paul a prisoner.

FELIX was not unkind to Paul; but some of Paul's warning reminders struck terror into his heart. His wife Drusilla was the daughter of Herod Agrippa I. She had been married to Azizus, King of Emesa. But Felix, with the help of a magician called Atomos, had seduced her from Azizus and persuaded her to marry him. It is little wonder that, when Paul presented him with the high moral demands of God, he was afraid.

For two years Paul was in prison, and then Felix went too far once too often and was recalled. There was a long-standing argument as to whether Caesarea was a Jewish or a Greek city, and Jews and Greeks were at daggers drawn. There was an outbreak of mob violence in which the Jews came off best. Felix despatched his troops to aid the Gentiles. Thousands of Jews were killed; and the troops, with Felix's consent and encouragement, ransacked and looted the houses of the wealthiest Jews in the city.

The Jews did what all Roman provincials had a right to do – they reported their governor to Rome. That was why Felix left Paul in prison, even though he was well aware that he should be set free. He was trying to curry favour with the Jews – but it was all to no avail. He was dismissed from his governorship, and only the influence of his brother Pallas saved him from execution.

I APPEAL TO CAESAR

Acts 25:1–12

> Three days after he had entered into his province, Festus went up to Jerusalem. The chief priests and the chief men of the Jews laid information before him against Paul. They urged him, asking a favour against Paul, to send for him to be brought to Jerusalem, for they were hatching a plot to murder him on the way. But Festus replied that Paul was under guard at Caesarea and that he himself would soon be leaving. 'So,' he said, 'let your men of power come down with me, and, if there is anything amiss with the man, let them make their accusations.' After spending no more than eight or ten days among them, when he had gone down to Caesarea, he took his place on his judgment seat and ordered Paul to be brought in. When Paul came in, the Jews who had come down from Jerusalem surrounded

him; they levelled many serious accusations against him, which they were unable to prove, while Paul said in his defence: 'I have committed no crime either against the laws of the Jews, or against the Temple, or against Caesar.' But Festus, with the desire to ingratiate himself with the Jews, replied to Paul: 'Are you willing to go to Jerusalem and in my presence to be tried on these charges?' But Paul said: 'I am standing at Caesar's judgment seat where I ought to be tried. I have committed no crime against the Jews, as you very well know; but if I have committed some crime and if I have done something which merits death, I am not trying to beg myself off dying. But if there is nothing in the charges of which they accuse me, no one can hand me over as a favour to them. I appeal to Caesar.' After Festus had conferred with his assessors, he said: 'You have appealed to Caesar; to Caesar you will go.'

FESTUS was very different from Felix; we know very little about him, but what we do know proves that he was a just and upright man. He died after only two years in office; but he died with his reputation intact. The Jews tried to take advantage of him; they tried to persuade him to send for Paul to come to Jerusalem; for once again they had plotted to assassinate Paul on the way. But Festus was a Roman, with the Roman instinct for justice, and he told them to come to Caesarea and plead their case there. From Paul's answer, we can deduce the malicious charges which they levelled against him. They accused him of heresy, of sacrilege and of treason. No doubt from their point of view the first charge was true, irrelevant as it was to Roman law; but the second two were deliberate lies.

Festus had no desire to get on the wrong side of the Jews in the first days of his governorship, and he offered a compromise. Was Paul, he asked, prepared to go to Jerusalem and stand trial there while he stood by to see fair play? But Paul knew that for him there could be no such thing as fair play in Jerusalem, and he took his great decision. If Roman citizens felt they were not getting justice in a provincial court, they could appeal direct to the emperor. Only in the case of a murderer, a pirate or a bandit caught in the act was the appeal invalid. In all other cases, the local procedure had to be halted and the claimant had to be despatched to Rome for the personal decision of the emperor. When Paul uttered the fateful words 'I appeal to Caesar', Festus had no choice; and so Paul, in very different circumstances from those of which he had dreamt, had set his foot upon the first step of the road that led to Rome.

FESTUS AND AGRIPPA

Acts 25:13–21

> When some days had elapsed, Agrippa, the king, and Bernice came to Caesarea to welcome Festus. As they were staying there for some time, Festus referred Paul's case to the king. 'There is a man', he said, 'who was left behind by Felix, a prisoner. When I was in Jerusalem, the chief priests and the elders of the Jews laid information before me concerning him and asked for his condemnation. I replied to them that it is not the custom of the Romans to grant any man's life as a favour before the accused meets his accusers face to face and receives an opportunity to make his defence against their charge. So when they came down here I made no delay, but on the next day I took my seat on my judgment seat and ordered the man to be brought in. The accusers rose and brought against him none of the accusations of crime which I was expecting; but they had an argument with him about their own religion and about someone called

Jesus who was dead and whom Paul insists to be alive. I did not know what to make of the dispute about these matters, so I asked him if he was willing to go to Jerusalem and to be tried there on these charges; but Paul appealed and demanded to be held for His Majesty's investigation and decision; so I ordered him to be held until I should remand him to Caesar.'

AGRIPPA was still king of quite a small part of Palestine, which included Galilee and Peraea; but he knew quite well that he owed his position even in that limited realm to the Romans. They had put him there, and they could just as easily remove him. It was therefore his custom to pay a courtesy visit to the Roman governor when he entered his province. Bernice was a sister of Drusilla, the wife of Felix, and she was also a sister of Agrippa himself. Festus, knowing that Agrippa had the most intimate knowledge of Jewish faith and practice, proposed to discuss Paul's case with him. He gave Agrippa a characteristically impartial review of the situation as it existed at that moment; and now the stage was set for Paul to plead his case and bear his witness before a king. Jesus had said: 'You will be dragged before governors and kings because of me' (Matthew 10:18). The hard prophecy had come true; but the promise of help (Matthew 10:19) was also to come abundantly true.

FESTUS SEEKS MATERIAL FOR HIS REPORT

Acts 25:22-7

Agrippa said to Festus: 'I, too, would like to hear the man.' 'Tomorrow,' he said, 'you will hear him.' So on the next day Agrippa and Bernice came with much pomp; and, when they had come into the audience-chamber with the captains and the leading men of the city, Paul was brought in. So Festus said: 'King Agrippa and all who are here present with us, you see this man, concerning whom the whole community of the Jews kept petitioning me both in Jerusalem and here, crying out that he ought not to be allowed to live any longer. I understood that he had done nothing to merit death. But when this man himself appealed to His Majesty, I gave judgment to send him. I have nothing definite to write to my lord about him. So I have brought him in before you, and especially before you, King Agrippa, so that, when investigation has been made, I may have something to write. For it seems to me unreasonable to send a prisoner and not to send the charges against him.'

FESTUS had got himself into a difficulty. It was Roman law that, if someone appealed to Caesar and was sent to Rome, there must be sent with that person a written account of the case and of the charges. Festus' problem was that, as far as he could see, there was no charge to send. That is why this meeting had been convened.

There is no more dramatic scene in all the New Testament. It was with splendour and flourish that Agrippa and Bernice had come. They would have worn their purple robes of royalty and the gold circlet of the crown on their brows. Doubtless Festus had donned the scarlet robe which a governor wore on state occasions. Close at hand there must have stood Agrippa's court, and also in attendance were the most influential figures of the Jews. Close by Festus there would stand the captains in command of the five cohorts which were stationed at Caesarea; and in the background there would be a solid formation of the tall Roman legionaries on ceremonial guard.

Into such a scene came Paul, the little Jewish tent-maker, with his hands in chains; and yet, from the moment he speaks, it is Paul who holds the stage. There are some people who have an element of power. Julian Duguid tells how he once crossed the Atlantic in the same ship as the physician and missionary Sir Wilfred Grenfell. Grenfell was not a particularly imposing figure to look at; but Duguid tells that, whenever Grenfell entered one of the ship's rooms, he could tell he was there without looking round, because a wave of power flowed from the man. When we have Christ in our hearts and God at our right hand, we have the secret of power. Of whom then shall we be afraid?

THE DEFENCE OF A CHANGED MAN

Acts 26:1–11

Agrippa said to Paul: 'You have permission to speak on your own behalf.' Then Paul stretched out his hand and began his defence. 'With regard to the charges made against me by the Jews, King Agrippa, I count myself fortunate to be about to state my defence before you, especially because you are an expert in all Jewish customs and questions. Therefore I ask you to give me a patient hearing. All the Jews know my way of life from my youth, which from the beginning I lived among my people in Jerusalem. They already know from of old, if they are willing to testify to it, that I lived as a Pharisee according to the strictest sect of our religion; and now it is for the hope of the promise that was made to our fathers that I stand on trial, that hope to which our twelve tribes hope to attain, earnestly worshipping God day and night. It is for that hope, your Majesty, that I am accused. Why should you judge it to be incredible if God raises the dead? It is true that I myself thought it right to do many things in opposition to the name of Jesus of Nazareth; and this I did in Jerusalem. When I had received authority from the chief priests, I shut up many of the saints in prison; and, when they were executed, I gave my vote against them. Often throughout all the synagogues I took vengeance on them and I tried to force them to blaspheme. In my insane fury against them, I even extended this persecution of them to cities abroad.'

ONE of the extraordinary things about the great characters in the New Testament story is that they were never afraid to confess what they had once been. Here in the presence of the king, Paul frankly confesses that there was a day when he had tried to eliminate the Christians.

There was a famous evangelist called Brownlow North. In his early days, he had lived a life that was anything but Christian. Once, just before he was to enter the pulpit in a church in Aberdeen, he received a letter. This letter informed him that its writer had evidence of some disgraceful thing which Brownlow North had done before he became a Christian; and it went on to say that the writer proposed to interrupt the service and to tell the whole congregation of that sin if he preached. Brownlow North took the letter into the pulpit; he read it to the congregation; he told of the thing that he had once done; and then he told them that Christ had changed him and that Christ could do the same for them. He used the very evidence of his shame to turn it to the glory of Christ.

The theologian James Denney used to say that the great function of Christianity was in the last analysis to make bad people good. The great Christians have never been afraid to point to themselves as living examples of the power of Christ. It is true that we can never change ourselves; but it is also gloriously true that what we cannot do, Jesus Christ can do for us.

In this passage, Paul insists that the centre of his whole message is the resurrection. His witness is not of someone who has lived and died but of one who is gloriously present and alive for evermore. For Paul, every day is Easter Day.

SURRENDER FOR SERVICE

Acts 26:12–18

> 'When, in these circumstances, I was on my way to Damascus with authority and commission from the chief priests, as I was on the road at midday, I saw, your Majesty, a light from heaven, more brilliant than the sun, shining round about me and my fellow travellers. When we had fallen to the ground, I heard a voice saying to me in the Hebrew language: "Saul, Saul, why are you persecuting me? It is hard for you to kick against the spikes." I said: "Who are you, sir?" The Lord replied: "I am Jesus whom you are persecuting. But up! and stand upon your feet! For this is why I have appeared to you – to appoint you a servant and a witness of how you have seen me and of further visions you will have; for I am choosing you from the People and from the Gentiles, to whom I am sending you to open their eyes, to turn them from darkness to light and from the power of Satan to God, that they may receive forgiveness of sins and a share among those who have been sanctified by faith in me."'

This passage is full of interest.

(1) The Greek word *apostolos* literally means *one who is sent forth*. For instance, an ambassador is an *apostolos* or *apostle*. The interesting thing is that a messenger of the Sanhedrin was technically known as an *apostolos* of the

Sanhedrin. That means that Paul began this journey as the apostle of the Sanhedrin and ended it as the apostle of Christ.

(2) Paul was pressing on with his journey *at midday*. Unless travellers were in a really desperate hurry, they rested during the midday heat. So we see how Paul was driving himself on this mission of persecution. Beyond doubt, he was trying by violent action to resolve the uncertainties that were in his heart.

(3) The risen Christ told Paul that it was hard for him to kick against the spikes. When a young ox was first yoked, it tried to kick its way out. If it was yoked to a one-handed plough, the ploughman held in his hand a long stick with a sharpened end, which he held close to the ox's heels so that every time it kicked it was caught by the spike. If it was yoked to a wagon, the front of the wagon had a bar studded with wooden spikes which caught the ox if it kicked. The young ox had to learn submission the hard way – and so had Paul.

Verses 17–18 give a perfect summary of what Christ does for men and women. (1) *He opens their eyes*. When Christ comes into people's lives, he enables them to see things they never saw before. (2) *He turns them from the darkness to the light*. Before people meet Christ, it is as if they were facing the wrong way; after meeting Christ, they are walking towards the light, and the way ahead of them is clear. (3) *He transfers them from the power of Satan to the power of God*. Once evil had control over people, but now God's triumphant power enables them to live in victorious goodness. (4) *He gives them forgiveness of sins and a share with the sanctified*. For the past, the penalty of sin is broken; for the future, life is re-created and purified.

A TASK ACCEPTED

Acts 26:19–23

> 'Therefore, King Agrippa, I was not disobedient to the heavenly vision. But first of all to those in Damascus, and to Jerusalem, and throughout the whole land of Judaea and to the Gentiles, I brought the message to repent and turn to God and do deeds to match their repentance. Because of this, the Jews seized me in the Temple and tried to do away with me. So then, because I have received the help of God up to this day, I stand bearing witness to great and small, saying nothing beyond those things which both the prophets and Moses said would happen, that the Anointed One must suffer, that as a consequence of his resurrection from the dead he must be the first to bring the tidings of light to the People and to the Gentiles.'

HERE we have a vivid summary of the substance of the message which Paul preached.

(1) He called on men and women *to repent*. The Greek word for *repent* literally means *change one's mind*. To repent means to realize that the kind of life we are living is wrong and that we must adopt a completely new set of values. To that end, it involves two things. It involves *sorrow* for what we have been, and it involves the *resolve* that by the grace of God we will be changed.

(2) He called on men and women *to turn to God*. So often, we have our backs to God. It may be in thoughtless disregard; it may be because we have deliberately turned as far away as possible from God's path for us. But, whatever the situation, Paul calls on us to let the God who was nothing to us become the God who is everything to us.

(3) He called on men and women *to do deeds to match their repentance*. The proof of genuine repentance and turning

to God is a certain kind of life. But these deeds are not merely the reaction of someone whose life is governed by a new series of *laws*; they are the result of a new *love*. Those who have come to know the love of God in Jesus Christ know now that if they sin they do not only break God's law; they break God's heart.

A KING IS IMPRESSED

Acts 26:24–31

> As Paul was making his defence, Festus cried out: 'Paul, you are mad. Much learning has turned you to madness.' But Paul said: 'I am not mad, Festus, your Excellency, but I am uttering words of truth and sense. The king has knowledge of these things, and it is to him that I boldly talk; for I do not think that any of these things are escaping him; for this was not done in a corner. King Agrippa, do you believe the prophets? I know you do.' Agrippa said: 'You surely think that you are not going to take long to persuade me to be a Christian.' Paul answered: 'I could pray that, whether it takes short or long, not only you but also all who are listening to me today were such as I am, apart from these fetters.' The king and the governor and Bernice and those who were sitting with them rose up; and when they had withdrawn they kept saying to each other: 'This man does nothing which merits death or fetters.' And Agrippa said to Festus: 'This man could have been released if he had not appealed to Caesar.'

IT is not so much what is actually said in this passage which is interesting but rather the atmosphere which the reader can feel behind it. Paul was a prisoner. At that very moment, he was wearing his chains, as he himself makes clear. And yet unmistakably the impression given is that he is the dominating personality in the scene. Festus does not speak to him as a criminal. No doubt he knew Paul's record as a trained Rabbi; no doubt he had seen Paul's room scattered with the scrolls and the parchments which were the earliest Christian books. Agrippa, listening to Paul, is more on trial than Paul is. And the end of the matter is that a rather bewildered company cannot see any real reason why Paul should be tried in Rome or anywhere else. Paul has in him a power which raises him head and shoulders above all others in any company. The word used for *the power of God* in Greek is *dunamis*; it is the word from which *dynamite* comes. Those who have the risen Christ at their side need fear no one.

THE LAST JOURNEY BEGINS

Acts 27:1-8

> When it was decided that we should sail for Italy, they handed over Paul and some other prisoners to a centurion of the Cohort Augusta called Julius. When we had embarked upon a ship of Adramyttium, which was bound for the ports along the coast of Asia Minor, we set sail, and Aristarchus, a Macedonian from Thessalonica, was with us. The next day, we put in at Sidon. Julius treated Paul kindly and allowed him to visit his friends and to receive their attention. We put out from there and sailed under the lee of Cyprus because the winds were against us. When we had crossed the sea, coasting along the shores of Cilicia and Pamphylia, we reached Myra in Lycia. There the centurion found an Alexandrian vessel bound for Italy and embarked us on her. When we were making slow progress for many days and had with difficulty arrived off Cnidus, because

the wind was unfavourable, we sailed under the lee of
Crete off Salmone. With difficulty we sailed along the
coast and reached a place called Fair Havens, to which
the town of Lasea is near.

PAUL has embarked upon his last journey. Two things must
have lifted his spirits. One was the kindness of a stranger, for
all through the voyage Julius, the Roman centurion, treated
Paul with kindness and consideration which were more than
mere courtesy. He is said to have belonged to the Augustan
cohort. That may have been a special corps acting as liaison
officers between the emperor and the provinces. If so,
Julius must have been a man of long experience and with an
excellent military record. It may well be that, when Paul and
Julius stood face to face, one brave man recognized another.
The other uplifting thing was the devotion of Aristarchus.
It has been suggested that there was only one way in
which Aristarchus could have accompanied Paul on this last
journey, and that was by enrolling himself as Paul's slave. It
is probable that Aristarchus chose to take this action rather
than be separated from him – and loyalty can go no further
than that.

The voyage began by travelling along the coast to Sidon.
The next port of call was Myra; but things were difficult. The
prevailing wind at that time of year was the west wind, and
they could make Myra only by slipping under the lee of Cyprus
and then following a zig-zag course up the coast. At Myra,
they found a ship from Alexandria bound for Rome. That
would have been a corn ship, for Egypt was the granary of
Italy. If we look at the map, we can see what a long way
round that ship had to take; but the strong west winds made
the direct journey impossible. After many days of struggling
against the wind, the ship slipped under the lee of Crete and
came to a little port called Fair Havens.

IN PERIL ON THE SEA

Acts 27:9–20

Since a considerable time had elapsed and since it was
now no longer safe for sailing because the Fast was
already past, Paul offered his advice. 'Gentlemen,' he
said, 'I see that this voyage is going to be fraught with
injury and much loss not only to the cargo and to the
ship but also to our own lives.' But the centurion was
persuaded by the master and the owner rather than by
what Paul said. Since the harbour was not suitable to
winter in, the majority proposed the plan of sailing from
there, to see if they were able to reach Phoenice and to
winter there. Phoenice is a harbour in Crete which faces
south-west and north-west. When a light southerly wind
blew, they thought that their purpose was as good as
achieved; so they weighed anchor and coasted close in
along the shores of Crete. But soon a tempestuous wind
called Euraquilo rushed down from it upon them. When
the ship was caught by it and could not keep her head to
the wind, we yielded to the wind and scudded before it.
When we had run under the lee of a little island called
Cauda, we had great difficulty in getting the dinghy
under control. They used their lifting tackle to get it on
board, and they frapped [undergirded] the ship. Because
they were afraid that they would be cast on to the Syrtis
Sands, they loosed the gear and away they were driven.
When they were making very heavy weather on the next
day, they began to throw equipment overboard; and on
the third day with their own hands they jettisoned the
ship's spare gear. When neither sun nor stars were seen
for many days and a great storm was raging, at last all
hope that we should be saved was taken away.

It is quite certain that Paul was the most experienced traveller
on board that ship. The Fast referred to is the Jewish Day of

Atonement, and on that year it fell in the first half of October. According to the navigational practice of the time, sailing was considered doubtful after September and impossible by November. It must always be remembered that the ancient ships had neither sextant nor compass, and in cloudy and dark weather they had no means of finding their way. It was Paul's advice that they should spend the winter in Fair Havens, where they were. As we have seen, the ship was an Alexandrian corn ship. The owner would probably have been the contractor who was bringing the cargo of corn to Rome. The centurion, being the senior officer on board, had the last word. It is significant that Paul, the prisoner under arrest, was allowed his say when advice was being taken. But Fair Havens was not a very good harbour, nor was it near any sizable town where the winter days might be passed by the crew; so the centurion rejected Paul's advice and took the advice of the master and the contractor to sail further along the coast to Phoenice, where there was a larger harbour and a bigger town.

A very unexpected south wind made the plan seem easy; and then the terrible wind from the north-east struck. It was a gale, and the danger was that if they could not control the ship they would inevitably be blown on the Syrtis Sands off North Africa, which were the graveyard of many ships. By this time they had managed to get the dinghy, which had been towed behind, on board, in case it should either become waterlogged or be dashed to pieces against the ship. They began to throw out all spare gear to lighten the ship. With the stars and the sun shut out, they did not know where they were, and the terror of the Syrtis Sands gripped them so that they abandoned hope.

BE OF GOOD CHEER

Acts 27:21–6

> Since they had been without food for a long time, Paul
> stood up in the midst of them and said: 'Gentlemen,
> you should have obeyed me and you should not have
> sailed from Crete and so you would have avoided this
> injury and loss. So now I advise you to keep your hearts
> up. There will be no loss of life among you, but only the
> ship. For this night there stood beside me the Angel of
> God, whose I am and whom I serve, saying: "Have no
> fear, Paul; you must stand before Caesar; and lo, God
> has granted you all those who are sailing with you." So,
> gentlemen, be in good heart! For I trust God that things
> will turn out as it has been told to me; but we must be
> cast upon an island.'

THE perilous state of the ship was by this time desperate. These
corn ships were not small. They could be as large as 140 feet
long and 36 feet wide and requiring a depth of 33 feet in order
to float. But in a storm they had certain serious disadvantages.
They were the same at the bow as at the stern, except that the
stern swept upwards like a goose's neck. They had no rudder
like a modern ship, but were steered with two great paddles
coming out from the stern on each side. They were, therefore,
hard to manage. Further, they had only one mast and one great
square sail, made sometimes of linen and sometimes of
stitched hides. With a sail like that, they could not sail into
the wind. Worst of all, the single mast and the great sail put
such a strain on the ship's timbers in a gale that often they
sprang out of position, so that the ship sank. It was to avoid
this that they undergirded the ship. That means that they passed
ropes under the ship and drew them tight with their winches
so that they held the ship together like a tied-up parcel.

It can easily be seen what peril they were in. Then an amazing thing happened. Paul took command; the prisoner became the captain, for he was the only man with any courage left.

It is told that, on one of the voyages of Sir Humphrey Gilbert, the sixteenth-century English navigator, the crew of his ship were terrified; they felt that they were sailing right out of the world in the mists and the storms and the unknown seas. They asked him to turn back. He would not do it. 'I am as near to God by sea', he said, 'as ever I was by land.' The man or woman of God is the one whose courage stands when terror invades the hearts of others.

HOPING FOR THE DAY

Acts 27:27–38

> When the fourteenth night came and we were drifting across in the Adriatic, in the middle of the night the sailors suspected that some land was approaching them. They took a sounding and found twenty fathoms. Since they were afraid that they would be cast up on rough places, they cast four anchors out of the stern and hoped for the day. When the sailors were trying to escape from the ship and were lowering the dinghy into the sea on the pretext of being about to send out anchors from the bow, Paul said to the centurion: 'If these do not stay in the ship, you cannot be saved.' Then the soldiers cut the dinghy's ropes and let her fall away. When it was nearly day, Paul urged all of them to take some food. 'Today', he said, 'is the fourteenth day you have spent waiting without food and have taken nothing. So I urge you to take some food, for this is for your health; for not a hair of the head of any one of you will be lost.' When he had

said this and then had taken bread, he gave thanks to God before them all and broke it and began to eat. All of them were in good heart and took food. And we who were in the ship were 276 souls in all; and, when they were satisfied with food, they lightened the ship by casting the corn into the sea.

By this time, they had lost all control of the ship. It was drifting, broadside on, across the Adriatic; and they could not tell where they were. In the darkness, they heard the crash of breakers on some distant shore; they cast out sea anchors from the stern to slacken the drifting speed of the ship in order to prevent being cast on the rocks that they could not see. It was then that Paul took the action of a commander. The sailors planned to sail away in the dinghy, which would have been quite useless for 276 people; but Paul frustrated their plan. The ship's company must sink or swim together.

Next comes a most human and revealing episode. Paul insisted that they should eat. He was a visionary man of God, but he was also an intensely practical man. He had not the slightest doubt that God would do his part, but he also knew that they must do theirs. Paul was not one of those people who were so heavenly minded that they were of no earthly use. He knew that hungry people are not efficient, and so he gathered the ship's company around him and made them eat.

As we read the narrative, into the tempest there seems to come a strange calm. Paul, the man of God, has somehow made others sure that God is in charge of things. The most useful people in the world are those who, being calm themselves, bring to others the secret of confidence. Paul was like that; and every follower of Jesus ought to be steadfast when others are in turmoil.

ESCAPE FROM THE DEEP

Acts 27:39–44

> When day came, they did not recognize the land; but
> they saw a bay with a beach, on which they purposed, if
> it was possible, to run the ship ashore. They loosed the
> anchors and let them go into the sea and at the same
> time they loosed the lashings of the rudder paddles,
> and they set the foresail to the wind and made for the
> beach. When they were cast into a place where two seas
> met, they beached the ship; and the bow remained fast
> and immovable but the stern was being broken up by
> the surf. The soldiers had a plan to kill the prisoners
> for fear any should swim away and escape; but the
> centurion, wishing to save Paul, stopped them from their
> purpose. He ordered those who could swim to throw
> themselves overboard first and to get to land; as for
> the rest, he ordered some to go on planks and some on
> pieces of the ship. So it happened that all came safely to
> land.

ONCE again, the fine character of this Roman centurion stands
out. The soldiers wanted to kill the prisoners to prevent
possible escape. It is difficult to blame them, because it was
Roman law that if a prisoner escaped, the guard must undergo
the penalty intended for the escaped prisoner. But the centurion
stepped in and saved Paul's life and the other prisoners with
him. So this tremendous story comes to an end with a sentence
which is like a sigh of relief. The ship's company was saved;
and they owed their lives to Paul.

WELCOME AT MALTA

Acts 28:1–6

> When we had been brought safely to shore, we recog-
> nized that the island was Malta. The natives showed us
> quite extraordinary kindness, for they lit a bonfire and
> brought us all to it because of the rain which had come
> on and the cold. When Paul had twisted up a bundle of
> sticks and placed it on the fire, a viper came out of it
> because of the heat and fastened on his hand. When
> the natives saw the snake hanging from his hand, they
> said to each other: 'This man must be a murderer and,
> although he has been rescued from the sea, justice has
> not allowed him to live.' But Paul shook the snake off
> into the fire and took no harm. They stood waiting for
> him to swell up or suddenly to fall down dead; and
> when they had waited expectantly for a long time and
> saw that nothing untoward was happening to him,
> they changed their minds and began to say that he was a
> god.

IT was on the island of Malta that Paul and the ship's company
found themselves. The Authorized Version is a little unkind
to the Maltese. It calls them the *barbarous* people. It is
true that the Greek calls them *barbaroi*; but to the Greeks the
barbarians were people who said *bar-bar*, that is, people who
spoke an unintelligible foreign language and not the beautiful
Greek language. We come nearer to the meaning when we
simply call them the *natives*.

This passage offers vivid insights into the character of Paul.
For one thing, there is the lovely and homely touch that he
was a man who could not bear to be doing nothing; there
was a bonfire to be kept alight, and Paul was gathering brushwood for it. Once again, we see that for all Paul's visions he

was an intensely practical man; and more, that, great man
though he was, he was not ashamed to be useful in the smallest
thing.

It is told that, in his youth, the American educationist
Booker T. Washington walked hundreds of miles to one of
the few universities which took in African American students.
When he got there, he was told that the classes were full.
He was offered a job at making beds and sweeping floors.
He took it; and he swept those floors and made those beds
so well that before very long they took him as a student, and
he went on to become the greatest scholar and administrator
of his community. It is only the small-minded individual who
refuses the small task.

Further, we see Paul as someone who was cool and calm.
In one of his bundles of brushwood was a sleeping viper,
which was woken up by the heat and which fastened itself to
his hand. It is difficult to tell whether this was a miraculous
event or not. Nowadays, at least, there is no such thing as a
poisonous snake in Malta; and in Paul's time a snake existed
which was very like a viper but quite harmless. It is far more
likely that Paul shook off the snake before it had time to pierce
his skin. In any event he seems to have handled the whole
affair as if it was quite insignificant. It certainly looked to the
Maltese like a miracle – but clearly Paul was someone who
did not fuss!

HELP AND HEALING

Acts 28:7–10

> In the neighbourhood of that place, there were estates
> which belonged to the Chief of the island, who was
> called Publius. He welcomed us and hospitably enter-

tained us for three days. It so happened that Publius' father was lying ill, in the grip of intermittent attacks of fever and of dysentery. Paul went to visit him. He prayed and laid his hands on him and cured him. When this happened, the rest of the people in the island who had ailments kept coming and being cured. So they heaped honours upon us, and when we left they gave us supplies for our needs.

It seems that in Malta the Chief of the island was a title; and Publius may well have been the chief Roman representative for that part of the island. His father was ill, and Paul was able to exercise his healing gift and bring him relief. But in verse 9 there is a very interesting possibility. That verse says that the rest of the people who had ailments came and *were healed*. The word used is the word for *receiving medical attention*; and there are scholars who think that this can well mean not only that they came to Paul but also that they came to Luke, who treated them through his medical skill. If that is so, this passage gives us the earliest picture we possess of the work of a *medical missionary*. There is a poignant thing here. Paul could exercise the gift of healing, and yet he himself had always to carry about with him the thorn in the flesh. Many people have brought to others a gift which was denied to themselves. Beethoven, for instance, gave to the world immortal music which he himself, being completely deaf, never heard. It is one of the wonders of grace that such individuals did not grow bitter but were content to be the channels of blessings which they themselves could never enjoy.

SO WE CAME TO ROME

Acts 28:11–15

> After three months, we set sail on an Alexandrian ship
> which had wintered in the island, the figurehead of which
> was the Heavenly Twins. We landed at Syracuse and
> stayed there for three days. From there we sailed round
> and arrived at Rhegium; and, after one day, when the
> south wind had sprung up, we made Puteoli in two days.
> There we found brethren and were invited to stay among
> them for seven days; and so we came to Rome. When
> the brethren had received news about us, they came from
> there to meet us, as far as Apii Forum and the Three
> Taverns. When Paul saw them, he thanked God and took
> courage.

AFTER three months, Paul and the ship's company managed
to get passages for Italy on another corn ship which had spent
the winter in Malta. In those days, ships had figureheads. Two
of the favourite gods of sailors were the Heavenly Twins,
Castor and Pollux; and this ship had carved images of them
as its figurehead. This time, the voyage was as prosperous as
the previous one had been disastrous.

Puteoli was the port of Rome. There must have been tremors
in Paul's heart, for now he was on the very threshold of the
capital of the world. How would a Jewish tent-maker fare in
the greatest city in the world? To the north lay the port of
Misenum, where the Roman fleets were stationed; and, as he
saw the warships in the distance, Paul must have thought of
the power of Rome. Nearby were the beaches of Baiae, which
was the 'Brighton of Italy', with its crowded beaches and the
coloured sails of the yachts of the wealthy Romans. Puteoli,
with its wharves and its storehouses and its ships, has been
called the 'Liverpool of the ancient world.'

For once, there must have been a churning in Paul's stomach as he faced Rome almost alone. Then something wonderful happened. Apii Forum is forty-three miles from Rome and thirty-three miles from the Three Taverns. They were on the great Appian Way, which led from Rome to the coast. And a deputation of Roman Christians came to meet him. The Greek word used is that used for a city deputation going to meet a general or a king or a conqueror. They came to meet Paul as one of the great ones of the earth; and he thanked God and took courage. What was it that so especially lifted up his heart? Surely it was the sudden realization that he was far from being alone.

Christians are never alone. (1) They have the consciousness of the unseen cloud of witnesses around and about them. (2) They have the consciousness of belonging to a worldwide fellowship. (3) They have the consciousness that wherever they go there is God. (4) They have the certainty that their risen Lord is with them.

UNSYMPATHETIC JEWS

Acts 28:16–29

> When we arrived in Rome, permission was given to Paul to stay in his own house with the soldier who was his guard. After three days, he invited the leaders of the Jews to come to see him. When they had assembled, he proceeded to say: 'Brethren, although I have done nothing against the People or against our ancestral customs, I was given over as a prisoner into the hands of the Romans from Jerusalem. When the Romans had investigated my case, they wished to release me because there were no grounds which could be made a capital charge against me. When the Jews objected to my

release, I was compelled to appeal to Caesar, not that I
had any accusation to make against my nation. It is for
this reason that I have invited you to come to see me
and talk things over with me, for it is for the hope of
Israel that I am wearing this chain.' They said to him:
'We have received no letter about you from Judaea, and
none of the brethren has arrived to report or say anything
evil about you. We think it right to hear from you what
opinions you hold, for, regarding this party of yours, it
is a known fact to us that everywhere it is objected to.'
They fixed a day for him, and a considerable number of
them came to accept his hospitality. He expounded the
matter to them, testifying concerning the kingdom of
God and trying, from early morning until evening, to
persuade them about Jesus with arguments based on the
law of Moses and the Prophets. Some were convinced
by what he said, and some refused to believe. When
they could not agree with one another, they began to
break up after Paul had made one last statement: 'It was
rightly,' he said, 'that the Holy Spirit spoke to your
fathers through the prophet Isaiah saying: "Go to this
people and say: 'You will certainly hear and you will
surely not understand; you will certainly look and you
will surely not see; for the heart of this people has grown
heavily insensitive and they hear dully with their ears
and they have closed their eyes, so that they cannot see
with their eyes and hear with their ears and understand
with their hearts and turn that I should heal them.'" Let
it be known to you, this salvation of God has been sent
out to the Gentiles; and it is they who will hear.'

THERE is something infinitely wonderful in the fact that to the
end of the day, wherever he went, Paul began with the Jews.
For rather more than thirty years now, they had been doing
everything they could to hinder him, to undo his work and
even to kill him – and still it is to them first that he offers his

message. Is there any example of hope that cannot be defeated and love that cannot be conquered to match this act of Paul when, in Rome too, he preached first to the Jews?

In the end, he comes to a conclusion implied in his quotation from Isaiah. It is that this too is the work of God; this rejection of Jesus by the Jews is the very thing which has opened the door to the Gentiles. There is a purpose in everything; at the helm of things is the unseen pilot – God. The door which the Jews shut was the door that opened to the Gentiles; and even that is not the end, because some time, at the end of the day, there will be one flock and one shepherd.

FREELY AND WITHOUT HINDRANCE

Acts 28:30–1

> For the space of two whole years, Paul remained there, earning his own living; and it was his custom to receive all who came to him, preaching the kingdom of God and teaching them the facts about the Lord Jesus Christ – with complete freedom of speech and without let or hindrance.

To the end of the day, Paul is Paul. The Authorized Version is misleading on one point. It says that for two years he lived in his own rented house. The real meaning is that he lived at his own expense, that he earned his own living. Even in prison, his own two hands supplied his needs; and he was not idle in other respects. It was there in prison that he wrote the letters to the Philippians, to the Ephesians, to the Colossians and to Philemon. Nor was he ever altogether alone. Luke and Aristarchus had come with him, and Luke remained to the end (2 Timothy 4:11). Timothy was often with him (Philippians 1:1; Colossians 1:1; Philemon 1).

Sometimes Tychicus was with him (Ephesians 6:21). For a while, he had the company of Epaphroditus (Philippians 4:18). And sometimes Mark was with him (Colossians 4:10).

Nor was it wasted time. He tells the Philippians that all this has happened for the furtherance of the gospel (Philippians 1:12). That was particularly so because his imprisonment was known throughout all the praetorian guard (Philippians 1:13). He was in his own private lodging, but night and day a soldier was with him (Acts 28:16). These headquarters soldiers were members of the hand-picked troops of the emperor, the praetorian guard. In two years, many of them must have spent long days and nights with Paul; and many of them must have gone from guard duty with a heart filled with Christ.

And so the Book of Acts comes to an end with a shout of triumph. In the Greek, *without let or hindrance* is one word – and that one word rises like a victor's cry. It is the climax of Luke's story. We wonder why Luke never told us what happened to Paul, whether he was executed or released. The reason is that this was not Luke's purpose. At the beginning, Luke gave us his plan for Acts when he told how Jesus commanded his followers to bear witness for him in Jerusalem and all over Judaea and Samaria and away to the ends of the earth (Acts 1:8). Now the tale is finished; the story that began in Jerusalem rather more than thirty years earlier has finished in Rome. It is nothing less than a miracle of God. The Church, which at the beginning of Acts could be numbered in tens, cannot now be numbered in tens of thousands. The story of the crucified man of Nazareth has swept across the world in its conquering course until now without interference it is being preached in Rome, the capital of the world. The gospel has reached the centre of the world and is being freely proclaimed – and Luke's task is at an end.